Contents

Endorsements

Health and Safety Executive

The Health and Safety Executive (HSE) recognises the importance of play in children's lives and for their opportunities to learn about risk. HSE is pleased to commend the *Managing Risk in Play Provision: Implementation guide*. Its application of risk-benefit assessments is a sensible approach to the health and safety management of play provision.

Barry Baker
HM Principal Inspector, Health and Safety Entertainment and Leisure Sector

Royal Society for the Prevention of Accidents

RoSPA recognises and promotes the fundamental role of play in children's lives. This guide allows play providers to ensure that they encompass appropriate levels of risk and challenge in their provision by balancing risk against benefit. This will allow children to exercise their right to play in more satisfying settings. Accordingly, RoSPA endorses the approach taken by this guide and commends it to readers.

David Yearley Head of Play Safety

PlayBoard Northern Ireland

PlayBoard the leading play advocate in Northern Ireland fully supports *Managing Risk in Play Provision: Implementation guide*. We believe and understand that children and young people need opportunities to create and engage in beneficial risk-taking within acceptable levels of risk. This guide, which adopts a practical common sense risk-benefit approach, instils confidence enabling providers to offer children challenging and stimulating play opportunities. We view this guide as a giant step forward and a powerful tool for all those tasked with the responsibility for the design, management and maintenance of play provision and services.   **Jacqueline O'Loughlin** Chief Executive

Play Scotland

Play Scotland welcomes this guide, which will be an invaluable tool for play providers who wish to put children's need for adventure and hands on experience of the world at the forefront of all they do. The risk-benefit assessment approach described here is practical and proportionate and will enable providers to drive forward innovative and inspiring places for play.   **Marguerite Hunter Blair** Chief Executive

Play Wales

Play Wales sees this guide and the development of risk-benefit assessment as a very significant and welcome step-change. In advocating that play providers balance the benefits of play against risk, this guide provides a tool which explicitly recognises and upholds children's need to create and deal with challenge and uncertainty in their play. It represents a common sense approach to providing for children's play.

Mike Greenaway Director

Association of Play Industries

The Association of Play Industries (API) understands the importance of delivering exciting and challenging play spaces for current and future generations. The API is a trade body representing over 85 per cent of the designers and manufacturers of playground equipment and surfacing in the UK. The API recognises the principles of the PSF guide and looks forward to providing inspirational play spaces for all our children.

Deborah Holt Association Manager

Fields in Trust

Fields in Trust welcomes the new guidance on risk management in play. The risk-benefit assessment adds an innovative approach to the long established and necessary technical risk assessments. We anticipate that the guide will contribute significantly to play areas, facilities and opportunities that better meet children's needs for challenge, excitement and exploration.

Alison Moore–Gwynn Chief Executive

ISRM

The Institute of Sport and Recreation Management (ISRM) welcomes this guide and advocates its use to our members and the providers of play, recreational and fun activities for children as an approach to risk management that also takes into account the benefits offered to children and young people as well as the risks. The ISRM, as a professional body that provides guidance and sets standards of service provision, also acknowledges and promotes the view that, while risk management starts from the position that outside expertise and advice are valuable, the ultimate responsibility for making decisions always rests with the provider.

Ralph Riley Chief Executive

KIDS

KIDS fully supports the principles of the Play Safety Forum guide. All children need to take some risks in life to grow and develop. We think this is especially important for disabled children, as they may have fewer opportunities for adventurous play.

Warren Koehler Regional Director, KIDS London

SkillsActive

SkillsActive, as an employer led organisation, believes that the approach outlined in *Managing Risk in Play Provision: Implementation guide* will help play providers to offer challenging and enjoyable play experiences for the children and young people they serve. We believe the guide's approach will assist staff in working to playwork principles, that it underlines the need for strong management and leadership amongst providers, and adds to the greater professionalisation of the sector.

Paul Bonel Director, Playwork Unit

Foreword by Baroness Delyth Morgan and Gerry Sutcliffe MP

The huge response to our recent *Fair Play* consultation shows that children and young people want to play outside. They also want bigger and better play areas with more exciting, varied and challenging equipment and activities available to them.

As we carried out our *Children's Plan* consultations around the country, we heard this message from parents too. Strong new evidence tells us that play is not only vital as part of a happy childhood but is also needed to develop skills that are important for success in life. The Government's Play Strategy responds to this, and sets out a vision for excellent play opportunities in every local area. We want all children to enjoy playing outside in safe, but exciting, environments.

Parents and children recognise that you can never make everything completely safe, and that a balance is needed between risk and fun. As we said in the Government's *Staying Safe Action Plan*, everyone has a role in making sure that children are safe to enjoy their childhoods. To do this we all need to strike the right balance between protecting our children from harm and allowing them the freedom to develop independence.

This *Managing Risk in Play Provision* guide sets out in clear, practical terms how this difficult balance can be achieved in play provision, through the decisions providers and managers make locally. We are very pleased to have worked closely with the Health and Safety Executive and other key partners to get this guidance right.

With the use of this guide and *Design for Play: A guide to creating successful play spaces*, we look forward to more exciting, innovative and challenging play opportunities being offered to our children and young people in every neighbourhood.

Baroness Delyth Morgan

Parliamentary Under Secretary of State for Children

Gerry Sutcliffe MP

Minister for Sport

Foreword by Robin Sutcliffe and Adrian Voce

In December 2008, the Government published the Play Strategy for England after an extensive consultation that overwhelmingly endorsed its vision of a public realm that is both safer for, and more welcoming of children playing out. This is an integral part of the ten-year *Children's Plan* that aims to make England the best place in the world to grow up. Part of the vision is that public play areas should reflect and respond to children's need for adventurous, challenging play opportunities.

The Play Strategy, underpinned by £235m of new investment, therefore asks local authorities and all those involved in the design and management of public play space to respond to children's need to take risks when they play, and to manage those risks within a framework of understanding the benefits that they offer to children as well as the need to protect them from serious harm.

This approach, fully explored and set out in this guidance document, builds upon a commitment made in *Staying Safe*, the Government's Safeguarding Strategy (DCSF, 2008b). This recognised that 'wrapping children in cotton wool' or minimising all risks, however small, for fear of litigation, was having a negative impact on children's play opportunities and their more general freedom to explore and encounter the world, appropriate to their age.

Research tells us that the uncertainty and the challenge of much of children's play is a very large part of its appeal to them but also that it enhances the development of their brains, making them more adaptable and resilient as they grow.

Staying Safe, thus embraced the principle that children should be allowed to take some risks when they play that had been set out by the Play Safety Forum in its position statement, *Managing Risk in Play Provision* (Play Safety Forum, 2002 and reprinted by Play England in 2008). That short document had broken new ground in recognising the conflict between the need for children to experience risk and challenge whilst playing and the need for providers to offer an acceptable level of safety. It also recognised that accidents were inevitable in the playground.

The influence of the statement has been felt internationally. Its sentiments have been reflected in the foreword to the revised European Standard EN1176 and following publication a European Play Safety Forum was formed that produced a similar manifesto. There is also anecdotal evidence that litigation resulting from accidents on playgrounds has reduced.

In 2007 the Play Safety Forum recognised the need to update the statement to give more specific guidance to practitioners and was delighted when the Government asked it to develop the guidance as part of the support materials to support implementation of the Play Strategy. The result is this implementation guide.

Once again, this guide breaks new ground, most significantly in formalising the balance between the risks of injury with the benefit of children experiencing risk in play.

It does this through a new process of risk—benefit assessment. It is a demanding document requiring politicians, directors and senior managers to be involved at a policy level in establishing the framework within which officers manage risk in play. It does not set out prescribed solutions, but demands that users, as experts, must make judgements, because through this process there will be greater flexibility in offering more open play.

As with the original position statement, the strength of this guide is increased immensely by the support of such a broad committee, not only embracing all aspects of the play fraternity, but also, and most importantly, the Health and Safety Executive. On this occasion, the authority of the document is further enhanced by the clear importance that the Government has attached to the issue.

We would like to take this opportunity to thank all the members of the Play Safety Forum for their continued — often critical but always positive and constructive — support. We would particularly like to thank Tim Gill, the lead author and Issy Cole-Hamilton, who managed the production, for their patience, enthusiasm and hard work. We believe the result will underpin current thinking about risk in play, enabling it to reach another level. And at a time of unprecedented national leadership and local investment in play we are confident that current and future generations of children will benefit in ways that will have a lasting impact.

Robin Sutcliffe

Chair of the Play Safety Forum

Adrian Voce

Director of Play England

PART 1

Introduction and legal framework

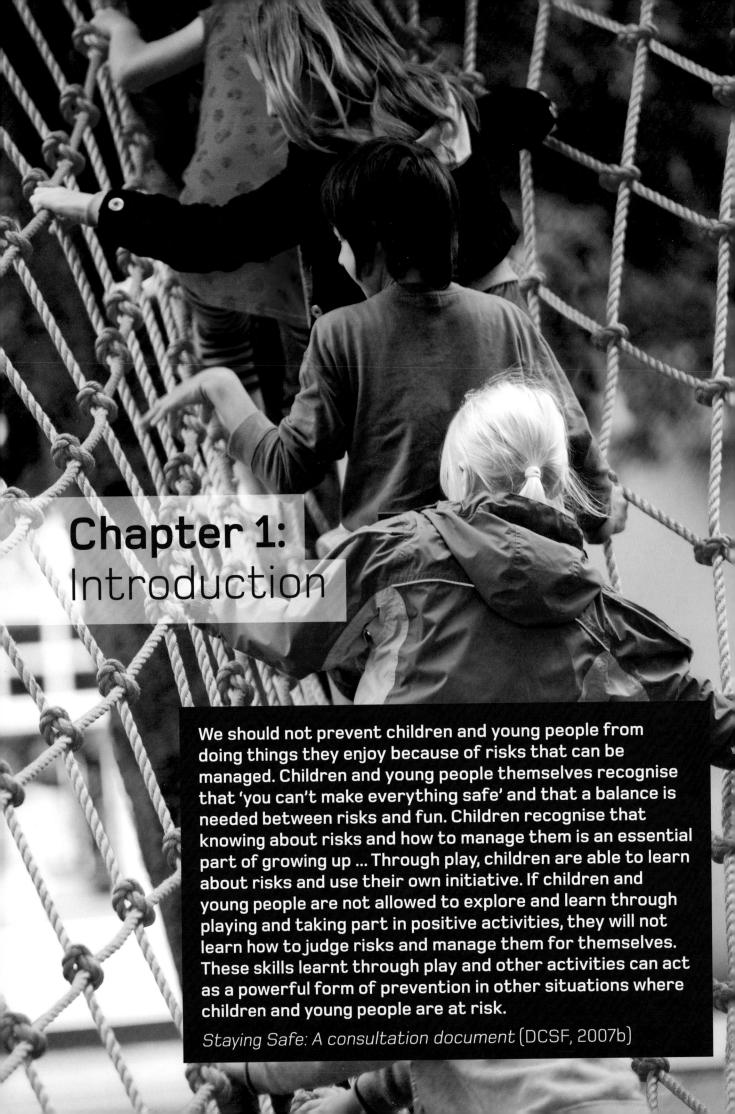

Chapter 1:
Introduction

We should not prevent children and young people from doing things they enjoy because of risks that can be managed. Children and young people themselves recognise that 'you can't make everything safe' and that a balance is needed between risks and fun. Children recognise that knowing about risks and how to manage them is an essential part of growing up ... Through play, children are able to learn about risks and use their own initiative. If children and young people are not allowed to explore and learn through playing and taking part in positive activities, they will not learn how to judge risks and manage them for themselves. These skills learnt through play and other activities can act as a powerful form of prevention in other situations where children and young people are at risk.

Staying Safe: A consultation document (DCSF, 2007b)

This guide shows how play providers can replace current risk assessment practice with an approach to risk management that takes into account the benefits to children and young people of challenging play experiences, as well as the risks. The guide is based on the Play Safety Forum's position statement *Managing Risk in Play Provision* (Play Safety Forum, 2002). It starts from the position that, while outside expertise and advice are valuable, the ultimate responsibility for making decisions rests with the provider.

This guide is written for those responsible for managing play provision, and for those involved in designing and maintaining such provision. The general approach should also be useful for those who manage other spaces and settings in which children play.

There is currently some confusion and anxiety about play safety. Many providers are unclear about their responsibilities and duties, and how these relate to the law, public policy, standards and guidance. More positively, there are signs of constructive debate and a healthier policy climate.

Who the guide is for

This guide is written for those responsible for managing play provision, especially unstaffed public play areas, and for those involved in designing and maintaining such provision. The general approach – though not all the detail – should also be useful for people who manage other spaces and settings in which children play, such as school playgrounds, parks, open spaces, civic spaces, adventure playgrounds, wheeled sports facilities, sports and leisure services, childcare settings, natural outdoor environments and visitor attractions. The guide uses the terms 'playground', 'play area' and 'play provision' referring to dedicated play facilities; the term 'playable space' refers collectively to all places where children's play is a 'legitimate use of the space' (GLA, 2008).

The guide is in three parts. Part 1 (this part) sets out the context, and gives the background and reasons behind the approach taken. Part 2 gives practical advice and guidance showing how this approach can be put into practice. Part 3 looks briefly at some policy issues. Readers are strongly urged to read Part 1 before turning to the practical sections. Government expects local authorities to have regard for this guidance and *Design for Play* in the delivery of play capital projects from the Children's Plan.

About this guide

This guide shows how those responsible for play provision can develop an approach to risk management that takes into account the benefits the provision offers to children and young people as well as the risks. It aims to help providers achieve two objectives that are fundamental in any play provision: to offer children and young people challenging, exciting, engaging play opportunities, while ensuring that they are not exposed to unacceptable risk of harm.

Fundamental to the approach is an agreed play policy that describes the organisation's position on offering opportunities for risk and challenge in the provision for which it is responsible. This forms the framework for a descriptive risk-benefit assessment which is supported by a technical inspection. These procedures work together to allow the provider to make well-informed judgements about the play opportunities, equipment and features they offer in play provision and other places where children play.

Risk–benefit assessment considers the benefits to children as well as the risks

The approach allows providers to address the two important objectives of play provision: providing challenge whilst offering protection from unacceptable harm. These objectives are necessarily in tension with each other. Children actively seek out chances to test themselves and develop their abilities: they are eager to get to grips with the world around them, so they will inevitably encounter some risk of harm, in any environment. What is more, adventurous play experiences help children learn how to deal with many of the everyday risks they will encounter throughout their lives.

For many children today, playgrounds are some of the few spaces that have the potential to offer interesting opportunities for play. The lives of children have become much more restricted and controlled over the last 30 years or so, as a result of cultural, social and economic factors. Hence, children's opportunities to play and explore their neighbourhoods on their own have decreased noticeably, and they spend more time under adult supervision at home, at school and in out-of-school services and activities. Many people argue that the built environment as a whole needs to be made more child-friendly if children are to be free to play outside as much as they would like to. However, play provision today has an important role in offering places where children can enjoy the kind of challenging, self-directed everyday play experiences that previous generations took for granted.

There is growing awareness that children both want and need to have challenging play experiences which involve a degree of risk. This awareness led to the publication in 2002 of *Managing Risk in Play Provision*, the Play Safety Forum position statement that provides the basis for the approach put forward here (Play Safety Forum, 2002).

Managing Risk in Play Provision summary statement

Children need and want to take risks when they play. Play provision aims to respond to these needs and wishes by offering children stimulating, challenging environments for exploring and developing their abilities. In doing this, play provision aims to manage the level of risk so that children are not exposed to unacceptable risks of death or serious injury (see Appendix 1 for full text).

Fear of litigation and a wider 'blame culture' can leave providers feeling exposed.

However, there is no common agreement about what should follow from this shared understanding, and many providers are unsure of how to put into practice the principles described in *Managing Risk in Play Provision*. There is confusion about providers' duty of care and how this relates to the law, regulations and guidance. Fear of litigation and a wider 'blame culture' can lead to providers feeling exposed, leaving them struggling to put into practice the approach to risk that they rightly believe is needed.

Playgrounds of all types are, by any measure, low risk environments for children and have been so for some years if not decades (Figure 1). This fact is one of the reasons for the approach advocated in this guide. To quote one of the authors of this guide:

Playground risk is exceedingly small in terms of fatalities, and in terms of lesser injuries is far lower than for most traditional sports which children are encouraged to engage in, and in any case about the same as the risk encountered at home. (Ball, 2007)

The comparisons take into account exposure. For instance, more injuries occur in the home, but children spend more time at home than in playgrounds.

Figure 1: Non-fatal injury rate based on A&E attendances

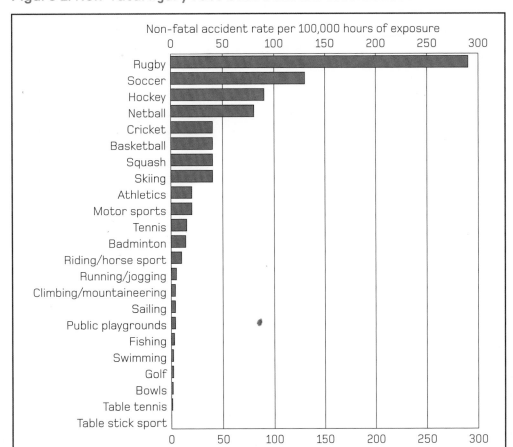

Figure 1: Estimated non-fatal injury rates associated with different leisure sports in comparison with play. Injury rates are based on attendance figures at UK accident and emergency departments.

Source: Figure 1 adapted from Ball D (2000b) in *ABC of Sports Medicine, 2nd Edition.* By McLatchie G, and others (2000) ISBN 9780727913661/0727913662 © BMJ Books. Reproduced with permission of Blackwell Publishing Ltd.

Effective risk management is the job of play providers and managers who are ultimately responsible, ethically and legally, for the judgements made about their provision. Others can and should give advice and support, but the provider has the final decision. Risk-benefit assessment needs to be based on clear values and understandings, bringing the assessment of benefits and risks together and requiring an appreciation of the role and status of industry standards and guidance.

Considering benefits alongside risk as a basis for making judgements will be new to many but is essential if providers are to create and manage provision that genuinely challenges, engages and meets the needs of children and young people.

The provider is responsible for making decisions on risk-benefit which will be informed by the organisation's agreed policy.

Traditional adventure playground structures have offered play experiences that include challenge and risk.

Photo: A.P.E.S

Much of the practical activity around managing risk in play provision is carried out by people with specialist knowledge of the technical aspects of playgrounds, for example, potential head traps or the structural soundness of equipment. People offering this expertise, and the other guidance and advice available, need to strike the right balance between risks and benefits. However, it is the provider who ultimately makes the decisions and who needs to consider this advice in the light of the organisational policy on risk and challenge in play before making their judgement.

The risk benefit-assessment process should provide a sound and reasonable defence against liability claims and prosecutions.

Not all questions about playground safety need expert input: some can be answered by applying common sense and everyday experience. This guide should enable providers to be clearer about their responsibilities and about when and how to obtain and apply appropriate guidance and expertise. Providers who follow the approach set out here should also be able to mount a sound and reasonable defence against liability claims and prosecutions, and hence defend their organisation's assets and reputation.

Concern about play safety

Almost everyone agrees that confusion about safety and risk management is widespread. It is by no means restricted to play provision. In 2006 the Health and Safety Commission (HSC – the former governing body of the Health and Safety Executive, which merged with it in 2008) launched a campaign against what it called petty health and safety. This was in response to growing public and media concerns about its increasing intrusion into everyday life. Its website stated that sensible risk management is not about creating a totally risk-free society. It went on to say that some of the 'health and safety' stories were just myths, spread through misunderstanding or misplaced frustration.

Sensible risk management is not about creating a totally risk-free society. (HSE, 2006)

The HSC campaign pointed out that health and safety is sometimes used as an excuse to justify unpopular or difficult decisions but admitted that there was a grain of truth behind some of the stories. The HSC stated that it wanted to drive out needless paperwork, and that it recognised the problem of overly bureaucratic risk assessment procedures (HSE, 2006).

The evidence that providers are facing an increase in liability claims is mixed.

The reasons for this confusion are complex and a matter of debate. It is partly a response to the perception of a growing 'compensation culture' that makes providers fearful of their liabilities. In fact, the evidence that providers are facing an increase in liability claims is mixed. Some providers and industry experts argue that claims are being made for injuries that would not have been the subject of any legal action a few years ago. However, a 2006 House of Lords Select Committee found that 'no significant statistical evidence emerged to support the notion of a developing compensation culture' (Select Committee on Economic Affairs, 2006). Local authority risk managers report that claims from playground injuries represent a very small proportion of their caseload, and there is no evidence of any dramatic increase in numbers. Whatever the truth may be, providers are more aware of the threat of litigation than they used to be, and are understandably more anxious about it.

Confusion may also arise from difficulties in applying workplace risk management systems to play and other public settings. The primary aim of health and safety in the workplace is reducing risk. It has been argued that these principles cannot be applied without modification and thought to play provision, where the focus is on providing a variety of experiences, some of which may be challenging and involve risk.

Children adapt the way they use play equipment. Part of the thrill of this slide for these girls is to go down head first.

Photo: Play England/ Alan Finlay

Providers need to use existing standards within the context of their local play policy and with reference to the needs of local children.

Concerns have also been raised about the inflexible interpretation and use of industry standards by some practitioners. There is undoubtedly confusion about the role and use of these standards, and legitimate questions can be asked about their scope and content (see Chapter 3). However, the emergence of more exciting, challenging equipment in recent years, shows that the standards themselves are not the primary source of the confusion. In some other European countries, where the same standards apply, playground design appears to offer children more challenging play opportunities. Providers need to use standards within the context of their local play policy, with reference to the needs of local children, and this guide aims to show how this can be done.

Some people argue that society is confused at a more fundamental level about the kinds of experiences children need if they are to learn and grow (Gill, 2007). Wider changes in public sector service delivery have also played a part. Shrinking budgets and the shift from direct provision to sub-contracting and outsourcing can make it more difficult for providers to put values and policies into practice.

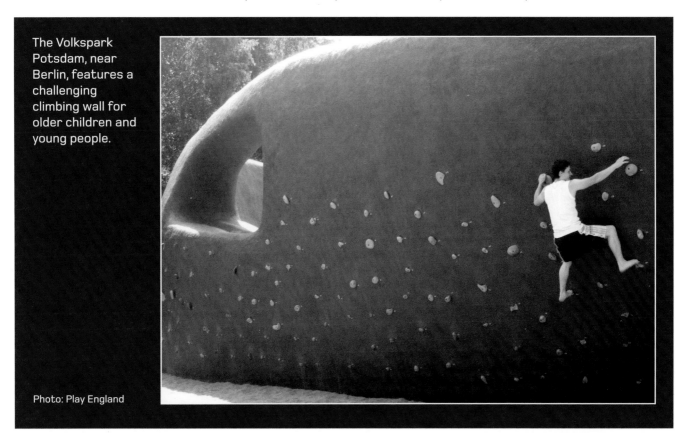

The Volkspark Potsdam, near Berlin, features a challenging climbing wall for older children and young people.

Photo: Play England

Most parents accept that their children need to learn about different types of risk and challenge as they grow up.

Parents' fears for their children's safety are sometimes cited as a reason for not offering children potentially risky play opportunities. Some parents and carers are more anxious than others, and they will not always agree about whether or not it is acceptable for their child to be exposed to a given risk. However, most parents are well aware that their children need to learn how to deal with many types of challenging situations as they grow up, and some can be seen encouraging children to take greater risks in playgrounds than they would without such backing (Ball, 2002).

Providers need to decide for themselves what level of risk is appropriate in their provision, because the type and style of provision must be responsive to local circumstances. This is one reason why industry standards, which necessarily have a one-size-fits-all format, need to be interpreted within the local context. This enables providers to include equipment or play opportunities that some more anxious parents might object to. However, simply reflecting the concerns of the most anxious parents, and altering playground design in an attempt to remove as much risk and challenge as possible, prevents providers from offering important benefits to the vast majority of children and young people. It may also lead more adventurous children to seek physical challenges in other, less well-managed environments, while others settle for sedentary activities.

Changing views

There is vigorous debate about risk in society generally. However, there are signs that the public policy climate may be changing for the better.

Children use play to test their limits and deal with challenging situations.

Photo: Play England

Risk can be creative and exhilarating, but some risks need to be managed.

In 2005 the Government set up a Better Regulation Commission (BRC), reconstituted in 2008 as the Risk and Regulation Advisory Council. The BRC's first report called for 'recognition that risk can be creative and exhilarating, whilst also acknowledging that some risks need to be managed' (Better Regulation Commission, 2006). These sentiments are echoed by *Staying Safe: Action Plan*, published by the Department for Children, Schools and Families (DCSF, 2008a), which states that 'childhood is a time for learning and exploring', and warns against wrapping children and young people in cotton wool.

Managing Risk in Play Provision: position statement

Within the play sector, the *Managing Risk in Play Provision* position statement has challenged the tendency to focus on safety at the expense of other concerns, including health and well-being. Much of this guide is based on the arguments and conclusions of that statement.

Managing Risk in Play Provision: Extract

Providers should strike a balance between the risks and the benefits. This should be done on the basis of a risk assessment. Crucially, this risk assessment should involve a risk-benefit trade-off between safety and other goals, which should be spelt out in the provider's policy. Given children's appetite for risk-taking, one of the factors that should be considered is the likelihood that children will seek out risks elsewhere, in environments that are not controlled or designed for them, if play provision is not challenging enough. Another factor is the learning that can take place when children are exposed to, and have to learn to deal with, environmental hazards. Play provision is uniquely placed to offer children the chance to learn about risk in an environment designed for that purpose, and thus to help children equip themselves to deal with similar hazards in the wider world. (See Appendix 1 for full text.)

The latest version of the European Standard for fixed play equipment promotes balancing risks and benefits.

The *Managing Risk in Play Provision* position statement has achieved significant recognition across the play sector, within Government and from those involved in studying and managing risk, including the Health and Safety Executive (HSE). It has helped to create a climate in which providers are prepared to offer more challenging play provision.

The statement has also influenced industry standards. The latest version of the European Standard for fixed play equipment explicitly states that it is concerned with balancing risks and benefits. This change should improve the decisions of inspectors, the courts and others. Other aspects of the standard echo the arguments in the position statement:

Risk-taking is an essential feature of play provision and of all environments in which children legitimately spend time playing. Play provision aims to offer children the chance to encounter acceptable risks as part of a stimulating, challenging and controlled learning environment. Play provision should aim at managing the balance between the need to offer risk and the need to keep children safe from serious harm. The principles of safety management are applicable both to workplaces in general as well as to play provision. However, the balance between safety and benefits is likely to be different in the two environments. In play provision, exposure to some degree of risk may be of benefit because it satisfies a basic human need and gives children the chance to learn about risk and consequences in a controlled environment.

BS EN 1176-1 Playground equipment and surfacing – Part 1: General safety requirements and test methods (BSI, 2008a)

Following representations from UK delegates, the section of BS EN 1176 on impact attenuating surfacing has been redrafted. In the 2008 version (BSI, 2008a) the European Committee for Standardisation (CEN) decided that advice on the use of grass should be given at the national level. The UK, like some other EU countries, has deemed grass to be an acceptable surface underneath free falls of up to 1.5 metres, subject to a risk assessment.

Government departments, the HSE and the CEN all agree that, for play in particular, an element of risk to the user is an inherent aspect of good provision and that mitigating against all potential harm is neither possible nor desirable if that provision is to fulfil one of its main purposes.

Risk–benefit analysis means that the provider weighs, with equal consideration, the duty to protect children from avoidable serious harm and the duty to provide them with stimulating, adventurous play opportunities.

Children in South Gloucestershire are introduced to fire play in a controlled environment by play rangers from Children's Playlink.

Photo: Play England/ Philip Wolmuth

This guidance is a response to these issues, and its approach is therefore one of informed risk-benefit analysis. This means that the provider weighs, with equal consideration, the duty to protect children from avoidable serious harm and the duty to provide them with stimulating, adventurous play opportunities.

Put simply, the challenge is to let children take risks when they play, without putting them in undue danger of serious harm.

The *Managing Risk in Play Provision* position statement has also influenced safety policy debates in other sectors. In 2005, the Institute of Sports and Recreation Management, one of the members of the Play Safety Forum, rejected calls for children to have one-to-one adult supervision in public swimming pools, even though such guidance was intended to lower the chances of a child drowning in a pool. It did so in part because it argued that this might mean fewer children getting the chance to learn to swim in the relatively safe environment of a pool, resulting in more children and adults being unable to swim and so potentially at greater risk of drowning.

Chapter 2:
Legal and public policy context

Children need to take risks to learn how to manage risks. This is an essential part of growing up, and play is one of the most important ways in which they develop this vital skill. Riding a bicycle, climbing a scramble net, or pushing a friend on a swing all involve risk. It is essential that we do not try and remove all the risk from play or wrap children in cotton wool.

Fair Play: A consultation on the play strategy (DCSF, 2008b)

This chapter summarises the legal and policy context of risk management in play provision. In law, the governing body of a provider is ultimately responsible and accountable for decisions taken, even where these are based on the opinions or expertise of others.

Play provision is deemed to be governed by the Health and Safety at Work etc Act 1974 and the Occupiers' Liability Acts 1957 and 1984. These statutes impose a duty of care on providers and occupiers, captured in the notion of 'reasonableness'. Regulations require providers to carry out appropriate risk assessments.

Play provision also has to meet the requirements of the Disability Discrimination Act 1995 and other directives such as the Disability Equality Duty 2006. These do not alter the basic duty of care.

Public policy in the UK aims to promote the wider public interest. This involves balancing a range of considerations, of which reducing adverse outcomes such as injuries is just one (HM Treasury, 2003).

The phrase 'safety is paramount' is a familiar one, and is often used by politicians, public service managers and company directors. Likewise, managers and service providers may also say: 'Our aim is to eliminate risk' or 'Our objective is to minimise risk.' In most circumstances these statements are not true. They rarely describe how service and management decisions are made, nor do they describe how they should be made. They state neither what is required by the law nor how public policy works.

Managing risk in public spaces is essentially a value-based activity. It requires the risk of harm from an activity to be weighed up against the benefits, which might be quite different in nature. Judgements about how risks have been managed can be challenged, for instance in the courts. However, the process is neither mechanistic nor entirely objective. Different people may hold different, incompatible but nevertheless justifiable positions about the acceptability of many risks, especially those encountered in everyday life. Empirical evidence and technical data may help with such judgements, but the final decision will need to go beyond such evidence.

A provider might decide to offer play opportunities that increase the likelihood of injuries or other adverse outcomes within the playground because overall these possibilities are outweighed by benefits to children and young people. For example, a local authority with large numbers of teenagers looking for adventurous activities may legitimately build play provision that is particularly physically challenging. Similarly, in a densely populated, highly urbanised neighbourhood with little green space and a high proportion of young families, a provider may create play spaces with trees, bushes and other plants, along with sand and water, to compensate for the lack of other natural outdoor environments.

The play provider's governing body – the board, council, managing directors, committee or management committee – is ultimately responsible and accountable for decisions about risk management, even where these are based on the opinions or expertise of others. In this sense, the legal position of the top decision-making body of any provider is similar to that of charity trustees. While they are free to seek guidance from professionals – and in many circumstances would be strongly advised to do so – the final say is theirs, whatever the type, size or scope of the provider.

Evergreen Adventure Playground located in a densely populated part of Hackney features a natural play area and pond.

Photo: Play England

The legal position

In legal terms, play provision is governed by the Health and Safety at Work etc Act 1974 and the Occupiers' Liability Acts 1957 and 1984. These Acts impose a duty of care on providers and occupiers. In the case of the Health and Safety at Work etc Act, breaches of this duty of care are a criminal offence. By contrast, the Occupiers' Liability Act provides the legal basis for civil claims but not criminal convictions. In practice, both these pieces of legislation imply a similar level of care for providers, captured in the notion of 'reasonableness'.

The Occupiers' Liability Act 1957 states: 'The common duty of care is … to see that the visitor will be reasonably safe in using the premises.' It also states that 'an occupier must be prepared for children to be less careful than adults.' However, court judgements show that, while the courts view children as being less careful than adults, they do not view them as careless, incapable or vulnerable in an absolute sense. As they grow up, they can be expected take on ever more responsibility for their own safety (Jones, 2000). There is no requirement under the Act to eliminate or minimise risk, even where children are concerned.

There is no legal requirement to eliminate or minimise risk, even where children are concerned.

Likewise, the Health and Safety at Work etc Act requires that risks be reduced 'so far as is reasonably practicable'. The legal requirement to carry out risk assessments implied by this principle was stated explicitly in the Management of Health and Safety at Work Regulations 1999.

These regulations impose a legal duty on providers to carry out a 'suitable and sufficient assessment' of the risks associated with a site or activity, and to act accordingly.

It is important to understand the meaning of 'reasonable practicability'. In summing up legal cases where the expression has arisen, judges have offered definitions. In one key recent case, Tomlinson v Congleton Borough Council, which went to the House of Lords in 2004, Lord Hoffmann said:

> ... the question of what amounts to such care as in all the circumstances of the case is reasonable depends upon assessing, as in the case of common law negligence, not only the likelihood that someone may be injured and the seriousness of the injury which may occur, but also the social value of the activity which gives rise to the risk and the cost of preventative measures. These factors have to be balanced against each other.
>
> (House of Lords judgment, 2003)

The Compensation Act 2006 emphasises the need for the courts to take into account the benefits of activities when considering the duty of care.

The goal, then, is not absolute safety. The law requires that safety measures should be implemented if the benefits they bring (in the form of reduced risk, and bearing in mind the severity of consequences) outweigh the cost, difficulty and other disadvantages of implementing them. In giving its support to *Managing Risk in Play Provision* in 2002, the HSE recognised this position, saying that it 'articulates the balance between the benefit and the need for children to play against the duty of play providers to provide safe play.'

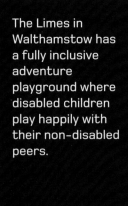

The Limes in Walthamstow has a fully inclusive adventure playground where disabled children play happily with their non-disabled peers.

Photo: Play England

The Compensation Act 2006, which was introduced by the Government in response to concerns about fear of liability, did not change the legal basis for liability claims or criminal proceedings. However, it did emphasise the existing need for the courts to take into account the benefits of activities when considering the duty of care.

Play provision also has to meet the requirements of the Disability Discrimination Act 1995 (DDA), which are to promote equality of opportunity for disabled people. Parents of disabled children – and disabled children themselves – are clear that they, too, want to have exciting, challenging play opportunities.

The voluntary organisation KIDS quotes the mother of a disabled young person who attends one of its playgrounds: 'The playground has given my son the space to experiment and take risks … the ability to meet physical and mental challenges; make and sustain friendships; get filthy and not care; sometimes fail but not give up; respect and be respected for whoever you are; and above all, be a kid and have fun! We need to stop telling our children what they can't do and show them what they can do.'

(KIDS, personal communication)

This guidance applies to disabled children and young people as well as their non-disabled peers. There is additional specific guidance available on inclusive play and the DDA, see Goodridge, 2008; ODPM, 2003; John and Wheway, 2004. However, it is clear that the DDA provides no barrier to the balanced approach to risk management proposed in this guide.

Taking risks is an integral part of play and risk cannot be eliminated from accessible play space for any child, including disabled and vulnerable children. Parents of disabled children frequently say they would rather their children encounter acceptable risk in play than be excluded. A balance has to be found between accepting that all children face a degree of risk in open and inclusive public play spaces and the pressures of the increasingly litigious climate in which we live.

(ODPM, 2003)

The European Union recognises the need for a balanced approach and accepts that risks cannot be eliminated.

In 2001 the European Union issued a general directive on product safety, which was incorporated into the UK's regulatory framework in 2005. It recognises the need for a balanced approach and accepts that risks cannot be eliminated (DTI, 2005). A similar message is contained in the Construction (Design and Management) Regulations 2007, which apply to construction work (HSE, 2007).

The primary procedural requirement is to carry out appropriate, written risk assessments.

The influence of the Health and Safety at Work etc Act and related subsequent developments, such as the implementation of the Management of Health and Safety at Work Regulations, has been to formalise the process of risk assessment, including making it a legal requirement to write it down (although to be exact, this requirement applies only to organisations with five or more employees). Hence, the primary procedural requirement under these regulations is to carry out appropriate, written risk assessments. There is no requirement under statute to comply with industry standards or guidelines, although these should always be considered.

Public policy

The fundamental approach to public policy decisions about public health and safety is to promote the wider public interest. This involves balancing a range of considerations, of which reducing adverse outcomes such as injuries is just one. This balanced approach draws on surveys and observations of public attitudes to risk and other things that they value. In that sense it reflects how society itself prioritises safety.

The 'proper management of risk', from a national perspective, is about balanced decision-making (HM Treasury, 2003; National Audit Office, 2001). Decisions should take account of factors such as whether the

existing level of risk is tolerable, the measures available to reduce the risk and their effectiveness, together with their cost, difficulty of application, and possible side effects or unintended consequences of the safety interventions under consideration.

The potential for unintended consequences is one that safety agencies have in the past sometimes underestimated. For example, one study showed that although a requirement for protective caps on medicine bottles did reduce the numbers of children admitted to hospital as a result of ingesting medicines, it also led to parents reducing their safety-related efforts because they over-estimated the safety of the products. In some cases entire medicine cabinets were left unsecured (Graham and Wiener, 1995). The Better Regulation Commission warns of the dangers of unintended consequences (Better Regulation Commission, 2006).

Government policy is clear that, for children, having opportunities to take risks is important for their learning and development.

The Government's policy on child protection, *Staying Safe: Action Plan* (DCSF, 2008a), and its consultation document on a national play strategy, *Fair Play* (DCSF, 2008b), are clear about the value of play in giving children the opportunity to learn and grow, in part through taking risks and learning from their mistakes. The Welsh Assembly Government's Play Policy takes a similar position (Welsh Assembly Government, 2002). Likewise, the Government's *Learning Outside the Classroom Manifesto* (DfES, 2006) affirms the importance of learning how to manage risks and deal with uncertainty.

How to manage risk in play provision

The approach taken by the *Managing Risk in Play Provision* position statement and by this guide mirrors the legal and public policy position as set out above. This position has itself been the subject of a robust legal assessment.

A play policy incorporating *Managing Risk in Play Provision* provides a framework for sensible decisions about risk in play provision.

In 2006 PLAYLINK commissioned Counsel's Opinion from the law firm Public Interest Lawyers. This tested the legal position of providers who have adopted a play policy that takes PLAYLINK's approach, which incorporates *Managing Risk in Play Provision*. Counsel's Opinion is not a legal precedent, unlike a judgment in the higher courts. However, it does give the considered judgment of a legal expert. In this instance, Counsel's Opinion clearly stated that a play policy incorporating *Managing Risk in Play Provision* provided a 'framework for sensible decisions about risk in play provision' and that it made 'cogent arguments for the allowance of elements of risk within play provision'. *Managing Risk in Play Provision* is 'very important to the policy as a whole' which includes a 'useful consideration of acceptable and unacceptable risk'.

Wheel parks may be inherently risky, but the benefits to children who use them, and the reduction in accidents taking place in other potentially more dangerous environments justifies their use.

Photo: Phil Doyle

The organisation's play policy and *Managing Risk in Play Provision* provide a sound basis for defending against liability claims: 'Where there has been careful risk assessment, resulting in a conclusion that it is permissible for play to involve a risk of injury, by reason of the resultant benefits, I am confident that Courts would be sympathetic to a Defendant, in the event of an accident and subsequent litigation' (PLAYLINK, 2006).

Many local authorities have (implicitly or explicitly) taken this balanced approach to risk assessment in their decisions to build facilities for skateboards, BMX cycles and other wheeled activities. All these pursuits are inherently risky, and it is inevitable that use of these facilities will lead to injuries, including some – such as long bone fractures and concussion – which might, in some circumstances, be labelled as serious. The decision to offer this type of provision goes beyond evidence of the risk of harm. It takes into account such issues as: the benefits for children and young people, including their overall health and welfare; the possible reduction in accidents elsewhere and the wider community benefits of providing places for young people to go and things for them to do. Design and construction standards give guidance on some of the more common types of facilities (BS EN 14974 and EN 15312).

Chapter 3:
Safety, risk, hazard and harm

The challenge for play providers is to incorporate these positive aspects of risk into their play provision, since one of its core purposes is to bring benefits and enjoyment to children and young people.

The framework, description and definitions used in this guide create the context for making judgements about what might constitute acceptable and unacceptable levels of risk. By offering definitions and a framework for thinking about safety, risk, hazard and harm, this chapter offers a balanced approach to considering the potential for children to be injured whilst taking risks in play.

As part of this process, the guide clarifies the terms 'risk', 'hazard' and 'harm', in order to clarify their positive as well as negative aspects. The guide advises caution in the unqualified use of the word 'safe' because this carries the unachievable and undesirable connotation that it is possible to exclude risk completely.

Definitions and descriptions

Safe

'Safe' or 'safety' is perhaps the most commonly encountered term in debates about children and risk, such as: 'Is this playground/park/ tree/public square safe?' There is no simple answer to questions like this, because the word 'safe' means different things to different people (Ball, 2000a).

This guide avoids unqualified use of the word 'safe'.

For some people the term 'safe' means that there is no risk of harm at all (which is very unlikely). For others it means that the situation complies with industry standards. For some it might mean that the level of risk is below some notional value that is regarded as broadly acceptable. Because of this ambiguity and confusion, this guide avoids unqualified use of the word 'safe' and recommends that providers and others do the same[1].

Hazard

Hazards are potential sources of harm. In its leaflet *Five Steps to Risk Assessment* (HSE, 2006) the HSE defines a hazard as 'anything that may cause harm, such as chemicals, electricity, working from ladders, an open drawer, etc'.

There is no action and no object that may not be hazardous in certain circumstances.

The word 'hazard' is sometimes used to imply that the source of harm is unacceptable and needs to be mitigated. This can be confusing

---

1 When talking about play sites in the Play Strategy, the Government uses the phrase 'safe and exciting' to refer to places where children feel safe and secure, but can still experience stimulating and challenging play opportunities, in line with the wishes of children and parents and the aspirations of this guide.

because, in fact, hazards are everywhere. There is no action and no object that may not be hazardous in certain circumstances, in the sense of having the potential to cause a degree of harm. People may trip over steps, slip on floors, walk into doors or fall from climbing frames.

Hazards have some value in that they can be an opportunity for learning.

It follows that the attempted removal or mitigation of **all** hazards is not only impossible, but also potentially damaging. If the world is, by its nature, full of hazards, people need to learn to recognise and respond to them in order to protect themselves. Part of this learning is through self-directed experience: gaining skills by encountering, assessing and responding to hazards as they arise. Hazards, then, especially for children and young people, have some value in that they can be an opportunity for learning.

It is impractical to treat all potential hazards with the same degree of seriousness. We need to make judgements about:

● which hazards need to be modified or removed

● which hazards might be acceptable or desirable, because of their benefits to children and young people

● what, if anything, is to be done about hazards that have been identified.

These children learn to negotiate barbed wire safely during a rural play session with Swainswick Explorers near Bath.

Photo: Play England/ Nick Turner Photography

Risk

In general use, the word 'risk' refers to the probability, likelihood or chance of an adverse outcome. In risk management contexts, the word tends to include a measure of the seriousness of the adverse outcome, as well as its probability. The HSE defines risk as the chance that 'somebody could be harmed by [a hazard] together with an indication of how serious the harm could be' (HSE, 2006).

This guide uses word 'risk' in a neutral way, without implying any judgement about acceptability.

As with 'hazard', the term 'risk' can also imply a value judgement that the chance is unacceptably high, as in the phrase 'that's risky'. Because of this, confusion can arise over whether or not a given risk is acceptable or not. This guide follows risk management practice in using the word 'risk' in a neutral way, without implying any judgement about acceptability. The following statements give some illustrations of the concept of 'risk':

● The chance (risk) that it will rain on your birthday if you live in the Midlands is about 15 per cent.

● The probability (risk) of a child (under 15 years) sustaining an accident in the home requiring attendance at a hospital accident and emergency department is about 10 per cent during a year.

● The annual risk of a child sustaining an accident involving playground equipment and requiring attendance at accident and emergency is 1 in 200, or 0.5 per cent.

Good and bad risks

Traditional workplace risk management involves identifying and, if necessary, mitigating hazards, in order to reduce the risk of an adverse outcome. This is different from play provision. Here, in many instances, the presence of a hazard — an unguarded vertical drop, a wobbly bridge — is potentially to be welcomed.

In a playground, bumps, bruises, scrapes and even a broken limb are to be expected as part of everyday life.

What counts as an adverse outcome is also different. In a playground, bumps, bruises, scrapes and even a broken limb are not necessarily warning signs of greater dangers, as they might be in a factory or an office environment. They are to be expected as part of everyday life for children growing up.

But what types of hazards, how much risk and what forms of adverse outcome are acceptable? This guide distinguishes between good and bad risks and hazards.

Good risks and hazards are acceptable and hold few surprises. Bad risks offer no obvious developmental or other benefits.

Good risks and hazards in play provision are those that engage and challenge children, and support their growth, learning and development. These might include equipment with moving parts, which offers opportunities for dynamic, physically challenging play; changes in height that give children the opportunity to overcome fears and feel a sense of satisfaction in climbing; and natural loose materials that give children the chance to create and destroy constructions using their skill, creativity and imagination.

Bad risks and hazards are those that are difficult or impossible for children to assess for themselves, and that have no obvious benefits. These might include sharp edges or points on equipment, weak structures that may collapse, and items that include traps for heads or fingers.

Therefore, good risks and hazards are acceptable in play provision and playable spaces. They hold few surprises. On the other hand, bad risks are more problematic, since they offer no obvious developmental or other benefits.

Most adults are competent at assessing good risks, partly due to their childhood experiences and observations of other children. No other training or expertise is needed to do this. Assessing bad risks, on the other hand, can require expertise. Deciding what load a structure can support, or whether or not a play structure has head traps, is a job for an expert. One benefit of industry standards is that they allow these bad risks to be identified, advised upon and periodically reviewed.

Deciding what load a structure can support, or whether or not a play structure has head traps, is a job for an expert.

As *Managing Risk in Play Provision* states, children have 'a growing ability to assess and manage risk which adults arguably tend to underestimate'. Most children naturally regulate their exposure to the good risks offered in play provision, such as the risk of falling from height. Deciding how high to climb, how far to jump and whether or not to succumb to peer pressure to do either, are all valuable experiences in learning to handle uncertainty and danger.

However, the distinction between good and bad risk is not always easy to make, and different people may draw the line in different places. For instance, unprotected falls from a height are arguably good up to a certain level, but if they are too high they become problematic. One relevant factor is the frequency of injuries. One or two broken limbs a year arising from a popular, challenging piece of equipment might not be a problem in a busy play space; in a small, quiet neighbourhood play area, though, it may be a bigger issue.

Deciding on what is and is not acceptable depends as much on the needs of children and young people as on the evidence of possible risk.

There are not usually clear answers to questions about where to draw the line between acceptability and unacceptability. It depends partly on evidence, but also on other factors like the age and capability of the user group, their desires and needs, and other considerations. Industry standards help to set reference points, but do not provide an absolute answer. Some mildly poisonous plants or berries offer both good and bad risks: they may add to attractiveness and play value, but they are also a hazard that some children and carers may not be fully aware of. It is almost unheard of for children to die or be permanently disabled from eating poisonous plants, but this has not stopped some local authorities and others from removing traditional plants from parks and public spaces.

Children's ability to risk assess is often underestimated by adults.

Photo: Play England

Harm

Conventionally, harm is thought of as exclusively negative. The dictionary definition revolves around harm being an injury of some sort. From this guide's perspective, it is unhelpful always to define 'harm' and 'injury' as negative. In daily life we respond to the concept of 'harm' in a highly nuanced way, particularly where children and young people are concerned. The phrase, 'That'll teach you!' is an acknowledgement that self-generated harm can be a valuable form of instruction.

Learning from experience involves encountering difficulty as much as pleasure.

Many bruising and painful encounters with reality are commonly understood as a way of 'learning from experience'. In other words, at least some injuries – and the hazards that might cause them – need to be valued for providing this chance to learn survival skills. Simulated risks (such as those in highly managed safety education projects, or virtual worlds) may offer some opportunities for learning about risk. However, children do not have the same imperative to identify, manage or learn from these risks as they would in the real world, since they know that there is no real danger.

In play provision, it is not always easy to decide what kind of outcomes are unacceptable or troubling.

As *Managing Risk in Play Provision* states, minor and easily healed injuries in play provision are not in themselves problematic. Ordinarily they should not be regarded as harm or adverse outcomes at all – unless they indicate the presence of an avoidable or bad risk such as a hidden sharp object, or a design or other fault that is likely to cause more serious injury. In fact, minor accidents will be common, due to the very nature of play and its role in child development. To quote BS EN 1176-1: '[C]hildren need to learn to cope with risk and this may lead to bumps and bruises and even occasionally a broken limb' (BSI, 2008a). CEN – the body through which the European play equipment standards are developed – makes a similar point in its Child Safety Mandate, which applies to a wide range of product areas and standards.

> An essential part of the process of a child becoming an adult is the need, and desire, to explore limits and to try new experiences. Minor injuries are part of every child's learning process and are a far more normal part of their lives than is the case for adults. (CEN, 2006)

At the other extreme, it seems clear at first sight that providers should do everything possible to eliminate the risk of fatalities or permanently disabling injuries. However, as *Managing Risk in Play Provision* also states, the reality is different. Tragedies can happen on playgrounds, as elsewhere, and the fact that one has occurred does not necessarily mean that the risks have been poorly managed. Over time, and given the millions of children who visit playgrounds, it is inevitable that, very occasionally, permanently disabling injuries or fatalities will result, without any failing on the part of the provider. Between these two ends of the spectrum, the occurrence of injuries like concussion or broken bones may or may not be a sign that risks have been managed properly.

To some extent there are agreed definitions amongst policy-makers about the types of injuries that are deemed to be 'slight' or 'serious', and these are used by health and accident prevention professionals (DfT, 2004). This suggests that there is an easy answer to the question about the level of injury that might be a cause for concern – namely, serious injuries. However, the definition of 'serious injury' covers a wide diversity of outcomes depending on how and where it is being used. It ranges from injuries that are usually relatively minor and easily-healed like cuts and shock, through more serious injuries which nonetheless generally result in full recovery, like concussion and fractures, to permanently disabling or life-threatening injuries (Adams, 1995).

Activities like football, rugby or cricket involve a greater risk of injury than playing in playgrounds.

Photo: Play England/ Philip Wolmuth

Many factors influence the type and severity of injury that might be tolerable or acceptable in a given context. As *Managing Risk in Play Provision* notes, activities like football, rugby or cricket involve a greater risk of injury than playing in playgrounds (Ball, 2000b). Yet these activities are widely acknowledged as beneficial, and there is little public or professional concern about injury levels, although rules and regulations may be periodically reviewed as attitudes to risk change.

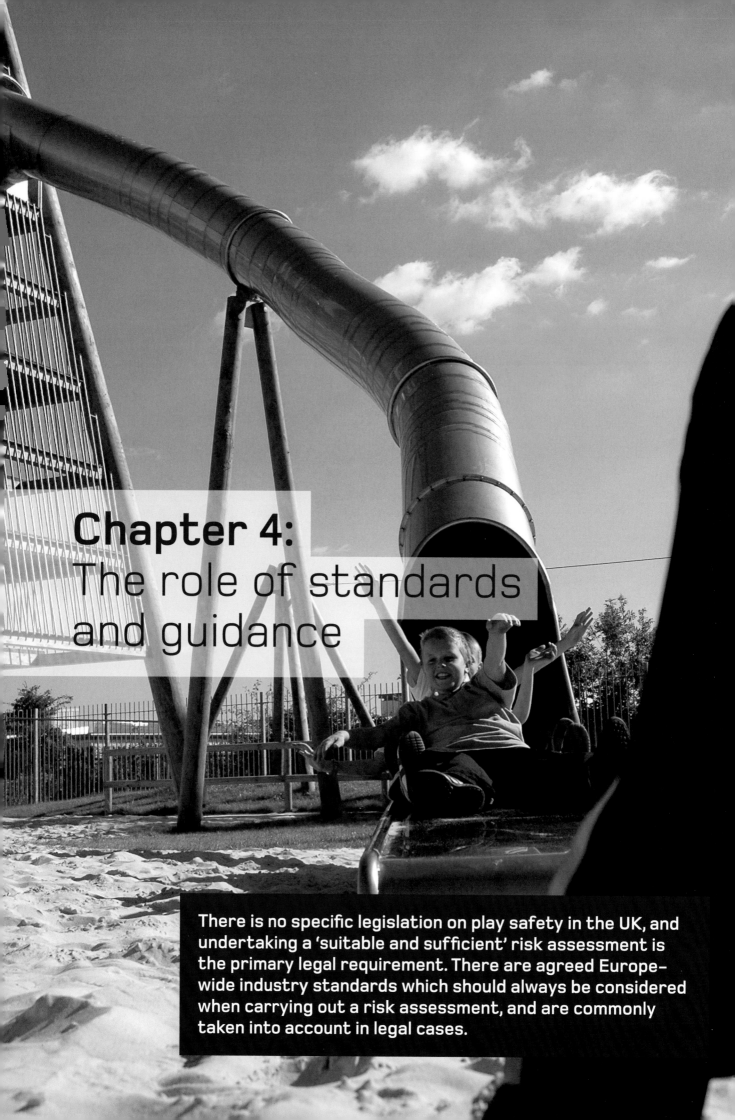

Chapter 4:
The role of standards and guidance

There is no specific legislation on play safety in the UK, and undertaking a 'suitable and sufficient' risk assessment is the primary legal requirement. There are agreed Europe-wide industry standards which should always be considered when carrying out a risk assessment, and are commonly taken into account in legal cases.

This chapter explores the status and role of industry standards and guidance. The primary legal requirement on providers is to carry out a 'suitable and sufficient' risk assessment. Compliance with standards is not a legal requirement, though they should always be considered.

Standards are important tools in managing risks, and give guidance about some difficult issues. However, a misunderstanding of their role and status has created problems in the past. The text of the most recent version of the key standard, BS EN 1176-1 (BSI, 2008a), may help in encouraging a more considered approach to how they are applied.

Alongside standards, other guidance, advice and information are available. This material should also be used amongst a range of tools available to inform play providers rather than as absolute requirements.

Compliance with industry standards is not a legal requirement. Counsel's Opinion, quoted in the previous chapter confirmed this. It stated that 'the proper approach to British or European standards is not to regard them as laying down a compulsory standard to be followed slavishly in all cases, but as a guideline demonstrating the general consensus as to what would constitute sensible precautions in any given case.' It continued: 'If a rational process of risk assessment, together with a balance of cost, risk and benefit can justify departure, then there would be no failure to exercise reasonable care' (PLAYLINK, 2006).

The key standards for play provision are BS EN 1176 (on fixed play equipment and surfacing), BS EN 1177 (on a method of testing for impact attenuating surfaces), BS EN 14974 (for wheeled sports facilities such as skate parks and BMX cycle tracks) and BS EN 15312 (for ball sports facilities such as ball games areas).

The tightening of an industry standard does not mean that older facilities suddenly and automatically become more dangerous.

These European standards are set by CEN, the European standards agency, and published in the UK as British Standards. They have their origins in earlier standards produced in the UK and other member states, and are periodically reviewed and amended to reflect experience and in response to changes in social expectations. In reality, however, the tightening of a standard does not mean that older facilities constructed to previous versions suddenly and automatically become more dangerous. Revised versions of standards BS EN 1176 and BS EN 1177 have recently been published in the UK (BSI, 2008a and BSI, 2008b).

The standards are drawn up by committees of experts and interest groups from some or all of the 30 member countries of CEN, which produce and revise drafts in working groups before these are circulated to a full CEN committee for agreement. They draw on a range of disciplines. These include engineering, physiology, psychology, product safety and social and cultural perspectives, alongside the views of manufacturers and providers.

Mile End Park in Tower Hamlets uses impact attenuating surfacing (IAS) enclosed within a raised boundary around climbing equipment.

Photo: Play England/ Alan Finlay

Standards help to set reference points about acceptable levels of risk, and give guidance in situations where providers might otherwise find decision-making difficult.

Standards are one key resource in the process of risk management. Their existence has, in the past, led to the removal of unacceptably dangerous equipment, raising the quality of construction, and more rigorous maintenance regimes. Used within the context of local needs, standards help to set reference points about acceptable levels of risk and to give guidance in situations where providers might otherwise find decision-making difficult. Reference to the standards in the past has resulted in some providers including pieces of equipment with manifest risk – such as vertical poles – that might otherwise have been omitted due to fear of accidents and claims.

However, in spite of the fact that standards are a guide, in the past a misunderstanding of their role and status has frequently led providers to take a purely mechanistic approach to risk assessment and management in play provision. Many providers regard the standards as being, in effect, a single and absolute requirement in risk assessment. This can lead to disproportionate and expensive corrective responses to minor failures, which have a minimal influence on safety. For example, some providers have wrongly concluded that they needed to remove equipment that has been used for years with no problems, because vertical drop heights are found to be a few centimetres above that specified in the standard. Using the standards as **one** of the considerations rather than the only tool would make it clear that such actions are not required in these circumstances.

Confusion can also lead those who design or commission play provision to focus exclusively on whether or not the items can be shown to meet the standards. In the past this has led to limited use of play features that are not specifically discussed in the standard, such as logs, boulders, hard landscaping, planting or changes of level. Instead there has been a tendency to choose equipment styles that fit most closely into those directly described by the standard, such as swings, slides, carousels, and multi-play and rocking equipment.

Chapelfield, near Cowie, makes use of boulders, sand and gradient variations that are not discussed in the standard.

Photo: Tim Gill

Left: ▶

Similarly, Wyvis Street Play Space in Tower Hamlets contains play features such as boulders.

Photo: Aileen Shackell

Right: ▶ ▶

Invermead Close Playable Space includes logs, boulders and a fallen tree.

Photo: Phil Doyle

Historically, the explanatory text in the standards emphasised their role in preventing injuries, with little or no mention of benefits. As a result, they did little to challenge the impression that injuries, and indeed risks of any kind, needed to be minimised. In fact all versions of the standards, going back to the first British Standard published in 1959, have (since this is unavoidable) balanced risks and benefits. The most recent (2008) version explicitly states that play value and other benefits have been taken into account in the standard-setting process.

The purpose of this part of BS EN 1176 is to ensure a proper level of safety when playing in, on or around playground equipment, and at the same time to promote activities and features known to benefit children because they provide valuable experiences that will enable them to cope with situations outside the playground. (BSI, 2008a)

While standards undeniably have a key role in guiding the approach to risk management, they are developed according to the current understanding of the best available evidence at the time of the review. As research develops, new factors come to light and these may not be reflected in the standard until it is next reviewed. For instance, since the standard on impact attenuating surfacing was first introduced, its effectiveness has been extensively studied over many years. Some findings suggest that it may not be as effective as had been anticipated (Gill, 2007; Eager, Nixon and Yearley, 2008), and that it does not meet the criteria for safety and health investment used in public policy decision-making (Ball, 2004). Findings about the comparative ineffectiveness of engineered safety measures are not uncommon (Jarvis, Towner and Walsh, 1995).

Risk–benefit assessment can be informed by information from many sources, including standards, safety and consumer organisations and research.

Alongside standards, other forms of non-statutory information are available to providers, including guidance provided by industry, safety and consumer organisations, and by research. Just as with standards, such material needs to be used within the local context and considering the needs of children, and as a guideline rather than a requirement.

Guidance from individual organisations may be less authoritative than the standards, which are subject to extensive debate and consultation. Such guidance simply represents the views of those agencies about what constitutes good or best practice at the time of writing. It may or may not be based on sound evidence. It may or may not be consistent with the policy objectives of providers or with over-arching public policy or societal aspirations. Finally, it may or may not correspond to what the courts decide is reasonable under the circumstances.

PART 2

Risk–benefit assessment

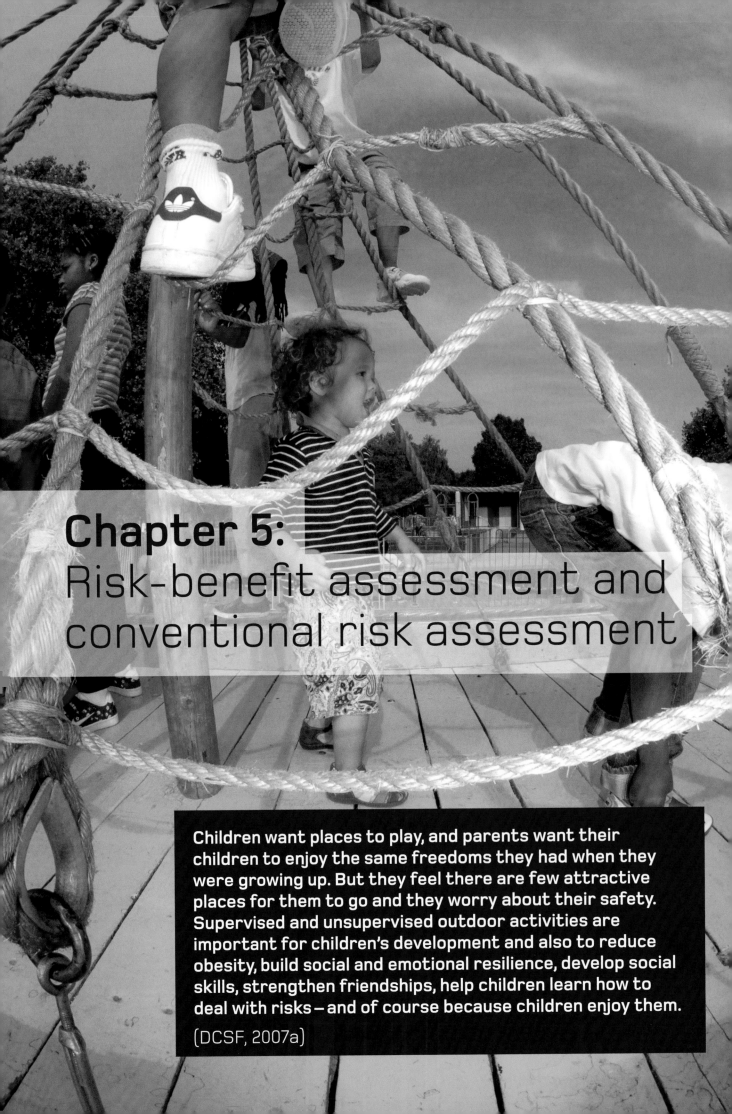

Chapter 5:
Risk-benefit assessment and conventional risk assessment

Children want places to play, and parents want their children to enjoy the same freedoms they had when they were growing up. But they feel there are few attractive places for them to go and they worry about their safety. Supervised and unsupervised outdoor activities are important for children's development and also to reduce obesity, build social and emotional resilience, develop social skills, strengthen friendships, help children learn how to deal with risks – and of course because children enjoy them.

(DCSF, 2007a)

This chapter proposes that all risk management in play provision should start with a clear play policy. This policy should set out the values, understandings, principles and criteria that form the framework for making judgements about play provision.

This section summarises the benefits and risks involved with play provision. It introduces risk–benefit assessment as an approach that satisfies the legal requirement for a 'suitable and sufficient' risk assessment, and argues that this should be done in a descriptive way, rather than by using any kind of scoring process.

Risk management in play provision involves balancing risks and benefits in a strategic way. Since the reason for providing play opportunities is their benefit to children and young people, the starting point – and most important consideration – for risk assessment and decision-making should be an understanding of the benefits that the provision offers.

The underpinning policy should clarify the values, understandings, principles and criteria on which judgements are based.

This guide advises that all risk management in play provision should start with a clear policy framework, which is best set out in a play policy. A play policy – as distinct from a play strategy – asserts the values, understandings, principles and criteria that form the framework for making judgements about play provision. It will include statements about the benefits of play for children and young people, and set out why providers should create play environments that offer, amongst other things, risk-taking opportunities. The policy should drive the strategy by stating the values that have been adopted.

A play policy establishes the framework against which providers can make judgements about reasonableness in risk management. It does this by affirming that risk is an inherent and necessary aspect of play. It makes explicit the duty of play providers to offer risk-taking opportunities, and asserts that, without such opportunities, children's and young people's happy and healthy development will be impaired. The policy must be formally endorsed by the relevant authority or organisation (PLAYLINK, 2006).

Benefits of play provision

Children want places to play, and parents want their children to enjoy the same freedoms they had when they were growing up. But they feel there are few attractive places for them to go and they worry about their safety. Supervised and unsupervised outdoor activities are important for children's development and also to reduce obesity, build social and emotional resilience, develop social skills, strengthen friendships, help children learn how to deal with risks – and of course because children enjoy them. (DCSF, 2007a)

The Government recognises the value of play for play's sake.

Photo: Play England/ Alan Finlay

The primary benefit of play provision is to give children opportunities to play, and in *The Children's Plan* and *Fair Play* (DCSF, 2007a; DCSF, 2008b) the Government recognises the value of play for play's sake rather than merely as a means to achieve other outcomes for children. The right to play is also set out in the UN Convention on the Rights of the Child. In fact, play provision can offer many different kinds of benefits to children, their families and the wider community, as set out in Table 1.

States Parties recognize the right of the child to rest and leisure, to engage in play and recreational activities appropriate to the age of the child and to participate freely in cultural life and the arts. States Parties shall respect and promote the right of the child to participate fully in cultural and artistic life and shall encourage the provision of appropriate and equal opportunities for cultural, artistic, recreational and leisure activity.

UN Convention on the Rights of the Child, Article 31

Table 1: Examples of the benefits of play provision

Benefit	Comment
Places to play	Children need and have the right to play, and play provision offers them places where they can play freely in the ways they choose, without direction from adults.
Space to meet and hang out	Children and young people actively seek out places to meet and hang out, and facilities for them are high on the list of local priorities in many neighbourhoods. There is widespread agreement that in many areas, young people in particular have a poor choice of leisure activities.
Space to have fun	Like adults, children need to enjoy their lives – to have times and spaces where they can simply have fun. Good play environments offer a wide range and choice of play experiences.
Support for parents and carers	Good, accessible play provision helps parents and carers to extend their children's play experiences. It can help to reduce conflict and relieve stress levels inside the home by providing other places where children can spend their time.
A community gathering point	Centrally located play facilities can bring different age groups together and foster interactions and connections between children, and between children and adults. Good multi-functional provision can help to build neighbourliness and a sense of community.
A chance to encounter nature	Children value the chance to interact with nature, and such experiences help them to appreciate the importance of the natural world and the environment. There is growing evidence of the health benefits of access to green, outdoor environments.
A place to make friends	The opportunity to make new friends and develop friendships is one of the most important experiences in childhood. In addition to this, such opportunities help children build their confidence and social competences.
Encourages physical activity	Most children are naturally physically active when they play out of doors. Comparative studies have shown that children can be as active in spontaneous outdoor play as in structured sport activities.

Benefit	Comment
Learning how to manage risks	Rich, challenging, engaging play environments allow children to test themselves and explore their abilities. They can learn the penalties of misjudging a risk – or simply having bad luck – in managed environments that reduce the likelihood of serious harm.
Developing a sense of one's abilities	Self-directed play experiences give children the opportunity to try out for themselves ways to solve problems and achieve goals, without the interference of adults. These experiences are likely to foster children's abilities and resilience.
Catering for the adventurous	Some children and young people actively seek out risky situations. Play provision can give them the chance to satisfy their search for excitement in a managed context, potentially reducing the risk that these children will spend time in truly dangerous environments.

Rich and challenging play environments allow children to test themselves and explore their abilities.

Photo: Play England

Risks associated with play provision

Table 2 sets out the main risks associated with play provision. As argued in Chapter 1, losses that solely affect the provider (such as loss of reputation, or losses due to legal cases) can be managed effectively by adopting the approach to risk-benefit assessment process described in this guide.

Table 2. Risks associated with play provision

Risk	Comment
Harm to users	Various forms of harm can befall users. These include physical injuries, psychological harm (for instance, from bullying) and criminal victimisation.
Harm or offence to others	Play provision can be disliked by non-users such as nearby residents who are unhappy about the presence of children or the noise they may generate. There is a risk of misuse of provision, for instance by street drinkers or petty criminals.
Loss to provider	The risk of litigation or adverse publicity cannot be eliminated, though it can be managed. The fear of such adverse outcomes is arguably one of the factors behind an over-emphasis on risk reduction on the part of some providers.

Bringing together the assessment of benefit and risk

As the nature of benefits and risks of play provision are different, it is difficult if not impossible to find numerical ways of measuring, comparing or weighting them against each other. While some benefits, such as health improvement, might be measured in terms of increased life expectancy, others, for example, increased self-confidence, cannot be. Likewise, actuarial data may be available for some risks, such as levels of some types of injury, or claim rates, but not for others.

The descriptive approach taken in this guide, called 'risk–benefit assessment', recognises that providers can make sound judgements about many of the risks and benefits relating to play provision but that they need to record their considerations and evidence base systematically. It is in legal terms a 'suitable and sufficient' risk assessment in the context of children's play, since it is a reasonable approach to the task of balancing risks against benefits.

This approach has been taken because other methods may be incomplete or restrictive. It might be theoretically possible to undertake risk-benefit analyses of policy decisions by, for instance, trying to calculate monetary values for risks and benefits. Such an exercise would mirror the kinds of analyses carried out by Government

Benefits are of a different nature from the risks and are not easily compared.

Photo: Play England

in reaching decisions about such issues as medical provision or major public infrastructure projects (HM Treasury, 2003). In practice, these are highly complex procedures, and are not appropriate for the more everyday decision-making carried out by play providers.

Alternatively, it would be possible to set out rules of thumb for assigning numerical values to both benefits and risks. Such scoring processes are fairly common in conventional risk assessment (though not benefit assessment, which is seldom done) in both the workplace and play provision.

Descriptive risk–benefit assessment attempts to overcome the drawbacks of traditional risk assessment.

However, for several reasons, this guide does not take such an approach to the overall assessment of risks and benefits. The most fundamental problem is that the benefits are of a different nature from the risks and are therefore not easily compared. It is also highly likely that any scoring process will vary widely depending on the scorer, and will not give reliable results. Assessment of benefits (and for that matter risks) also has to take account of local circumstances, and will draw on the provider's policy, which provides the framework for weighing risks against benefits. Such an approach is likely to lead to over reliance on paperwork and bureaucratic procedures, rather than the more considered approach needed in decisions involving value judgements.

Figure 2: The 'risk–benefit balance' (Ball, 2002)

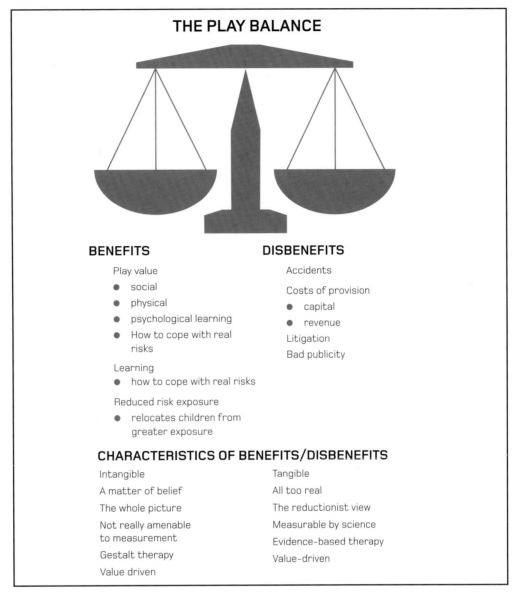

Figure 2: A simplified illustration of the problem faced by play providers. On the one hand, the good things associated with play are difficult to quantify, whereas the bad things – accidents, costs, litigation – are all too real.

Source: 'The Play Balance' from Contract Research Report CRR 426/2002 *Playgrounds – Risks, Benefits and Choices*. By Prof David Ball, ISBN 0717623408, Health and Safety Executive. Crown Copyright material is reproduced with the permission of the Controller of HMSO and Queen's Printer for Scotland.

Finally, most adults, through their own life experiences and everyday observations, have an intuitive grasp of how children of different ages play and gage with the world around them. Such accumulated wisdom should be a valued element of the risk–benefit assessment process.

Risk-benefit assessment highlights the implications of conventional risk assessment by explicitly introducing benefits into the decision-making process. In time, this should become the norm in play provision. Risk-benefit assessment is introduced in Chapter 6 and set out in more detail in Chapter 7.

Chapter 6:
How to manage benefits and risks

The section discusses the relationship between risk–benefit assessment and current practice. Very few providers will currently be undertaking activity at all the levels set out in this guide. A growing number are developing play strategies and policies, some of which include statements about the value of play, making reference to risk and the need for a balanced approach. These go some way towards the kind of policy framework required.

This chapter proposes breaking down the task of managing risk in play provision into four levels or modes:

- policy framework
- risk–benefit assessment
- technical inspection and
- dynamic risk–benefit assessment.

Three of these levels are applicable to all play provision; the fourth relates mainly to provision where supervisory staff are present.

Judgements about how to balance benefits against risks are ultimately a decision for the provider. Risk-benefit assessment achieves a 'suitable and sufficient' risk assessment which describes in a single statement the considerations of risk and benefit that have contributed to the decision to provide, modify or remove some facility or feature.

Technical inspection refers to the ongoing, largely routine, checking of play facilities for soundness, wear and tear, damage, maintenance and cleanliness. Dynamic risk-benefit assessment refers to the minute-by-minute observations and potential interventions by adults with oversight of children in staffed provision.

The role of 'common sense knowledge' and expert input are discussed. A set of questions is provided to help providers make the best use of independent expert advice they obtain.

The previous chapter outlined how risk management in play provision has to start with the strategic direction provided by a policy framework. It is only in the context of clear strategic objectives that the process of weighing up risks and benefits can take place. However, risk management clearly goes beyond merely stating values and policy goals. This chapter outlines the four stages of the risk-benefit management process: policy framework, risk-benefit assessment, technical inspection and dynamic risk-benefit assessment. Three of these levels are applicable in all play provision, and the fourth mainly in provision where supervisory staff are present.

The policy framework provides the context for risk–benefit assessment.

The policy framework should be the highest level of risk management. This should provide the context for the next level: risk–benefit assessment. This, in turn, should prompt technical inspections, and should take into account information gained from them. Where applicable, dynamic risk–benefit assessment should also take place, again informed by the higher levels of risk management.

Figure 3: How the levels of risk management relate to each other.

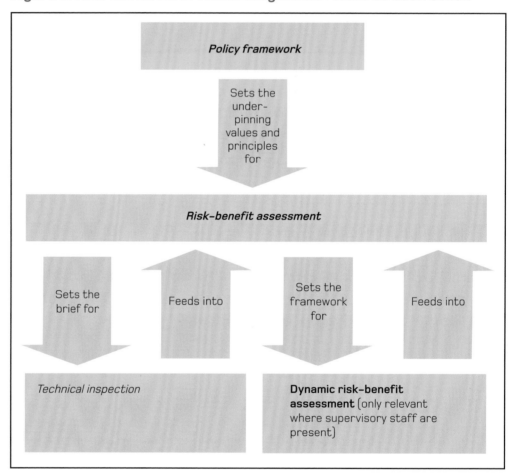

This table sets out some features of each of the levels of risk-benefit management activity.

Table 3: The risk management process

Type of activity	Style and function	Relevance to play provision	Some key competences needed
Policy framework	Framework establishing values, criteria, and understandings. Usually set out in a play policy. Should make explicit the rationale for establishing the positive duty of play providers to offer risk-taking opportunities for children and young people.	High. Essential for incorporating health, welfare and play value considerations into strategic and operational decisions. Context for making judgements in particular circumstances. Asserts primacy of risk-benefit assessment in making judgements about risk.	Grasp of value of play and play provision. Understanding of need for balanced approach.
Risk-benefit assessment	'Suitable and sufficient' risk assessments intended to promote a balanced approach to risk management, articulating and considering the benefits to children alongside the potential risks.	Essential, to clarify exactly why and how decisions about the nature and content of provision have been arrived at.	Ability to use judgement to deliver strategic objectives. Recognition of contribution of play and risk encounters to well-being. Appreciation of distinction between different types of risk
Technical inspection	Routine checking of facilities and prioritisation of repairs and maintenance.	Essential for installation and ongoing maintenance.	Technical knowledge of standards and ability to use judgement in applying them. Ability to assess risks that fall outside the standards against a coherent risk-benefit framework.
Dynamic risk-benefit assessment	Real-time on-site oversight and management of the play experience by experienced staff.	Not directly relevant to unsupervised settings but of high importance in staffed play settings.	In-depth knowledge of children, play and its role in their lives and in development. A full understanding of the different types of risk

All the levels of risk management work together.

In comprehensive risk–benefit management, all these levels of risk management work together. If the higher levels are neglected, there will be a vacuum for making judgements and decisions. In some smaller agencies, the same person may carry out tasks at more than one of these levels, and there may be a greater need for external expert advice. However, people in this position still need to be aware of the importance of this multi-level approach.

Policy framework

Agreeing an organisational policy framework requires setting clear objectives, and applying them to specific sites or services. It includes explicit value judgements about the importance of provision and what it is trying to achieve. This policy framework is essential because it helps to ensure that different people within a provider organisation, such as those delivering services, their managers and political leaders, all work together to take a coordinated approach, along with sub-contractors, health and safety officers, organisational risk managers and others.

Providers who do not have an agreed play policy framework are strongly urged to formulate one.

Providers who, as yet, do not have an agreed play policy framework, including statements on risk-benefit management, are strongly urged to formulate one. Arguably, the difficulties of play provision in recent decades have arisen in part because of a failure to promote an underpinning philosophy and to set clear policy objectives. Such policy documents, which should be publicly available, also provide one essential route to communication with parents, insurers, regulators, third-party inspectors, the courts and other interested parties. They contribute to a more stable policy background against which consistent decisions can be made. Guidance on play policy development can be obtained from PLAYLINK and Play England, in particular *Planning for Play* (Children's Play Council, 2006) produced to support the development of local area play strategies.

Risk–benefit assessment

Risk–benefit assessment is a 'suitable and sufficient' risk assessment that brings together an analysis of both risks and benefits. This guide proposes a descriptive form of risk–benefit assessment. This approach, explained in detail in Chapter 7, sets out in a single statement the considerations of risk and benefit that have contributed to the decision to provide, modify or remove some facility or feature. It should provide a reasonable and transparent means of describing decision-making processes and judgements.

Risk–benefit assessment, the law, regulations, standards and guidance

Play providers are legally required to carry out a 'suitable and sufficient' risk assessment of their provision, and to act on the findings. An assessment is a practical assessment of the benefits and the risks of the activity with a focus on **hazards with the potential to cause real harm**. It is not about creating a risk-free society, but about ensuring that **reasonable precautions are taken to avoid injury**.

Equipment standards, such as BS EN 1176 (BSI, 2008a) and other guidance, help in making decisions about what is reasonable. However, they are not compulsory, and risk assessment allows for consideration of other factors such as local circumstances, which might include the age groups catered for, type of demand, local environmental factors, health considerations and the use of non-standard or natural features.

Risk–benefit assessment is a method of risk assessment in which an evaluation of the potential benefits to children and others – for example play and social value – are considered alongside the potential risks associated with the provision. It allows providers to satisfy their legal obligations, while promoting a balanced approach.

This approach considers industry standards and other guidance in the light of local circumstances, and of children's need for more exciting and challenging play.

It is not about creating a risk-free society, but about ensuring that reasonable precautions are taken to avoid injury.

Photo: Play England

Risk–benefit assessment focuses on making judgements and identifying measures that manage risks while securing benefits.

Historically, risk assessment in play has often focused on injury prevention. However, there is now widespread recognition of the need to assess the benefits – including enjoyment, health and well-being – alongside the risks. Risk-benefit assessment focuses on making judgements about the risks and benefits associated with an activity, and the measures that should be in place to manage the risks while securing the benefits.

Risk-benefit assessment should form the framework within which judgements are made about technical inspection and dynamic risk-benefit assessment. Decisions about when and how technical inspection and dynamic risk-benefit assessment are carried out should be based on the judgement of the manager responsible for carrying out risk-benefit assessment. These decisions should consider guidance and standards on such questions as the frequency and nature of inspections, in the light of local circumstances.

Technical inspection

In this guide, technical inspection refers to the ongoing, largely routine, checking of play facilities for soundness, wear and tear, damage, maintenance and cleanliness. Technical inspection should alert managers to potential sources of harm. It can give an indication of the relative risk, and thus help in setting priorities for remedial action.

Technical inspection is an important part of this assessment and contributes to the evidence managers need for decision-making.

Technical inspection is informed by the play policy and risk-benefit assessment and, in particular, feeds into the assessment of risk. It is an important part of this assessment, because it should provide some of the evidence or raw data that managers need to use in their decision-making.

Technical inspection involves annual checks by trained, qualified playground inspectors, and more frequent, less intensive inspections carried out by people who require less technical expertise. A voluntary but widely used system of accreditation and training has grown up in the UK to provide support in technical inspection. Central to this system is the Register of Play Inspectors International (RPII), whose aims include promoting a consistent, high quality approach to inspection.

Whatever the level of guidance or technical training, inspection will always be a subjective process, and some providers and play equipment manufacturers have noted significant inconsistencies in the findings of different inspectors. Problems can arise when the providers or inspectors are not clear about the purpose or brief of a particular inspection or assessment. It also appears that some inspectors who are trained in technical inspections struggle when asked to advise on non-standard features in play provision.

Technical inspection traditionally gives information about compliance with equipment standards. Such inspections could, where appropriate, also cover the technical aspects of non-standard items, such as the load-bearing capacity of a tree – though often common sense and experience will be sufficient to make an informed judgement. Inspectors with a sound grasp of play and play values can also assist with risk-benefit assessment, where the focus is on wider, non-technical questions of risks and benefits in play.

Technical inspectors assisting with risk–benefit assessment must
have a sound understanding of play and play values.

It is vital that providers are clear about the distinction between
technical inspection and risk–benefit assessment, and that the
relevant knowledge and values are brought to bear in each. It is
ultimately the provider who must make judgments about risks and
benefits in play.

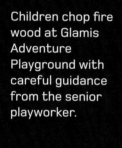

Children chop fire wood at Glamis Adventure Playground with careful guidance from the senior playworker.

Photo: Play England

Dynamic risk–benefit assessment

**Dynamic risk-benefit assessment refers to the minute-by-minute
observations and potential interventions by adults who have
oversight of children in staffed provision, such as school playgrounds,
out of school facilities and adventure playgrounds.** It is largely beyond
the scope of this guide, though it is worth highlighting, that for it to be
carried out well requires a sound grasp of how children learn and grow
through play.

Dynamic risk-benefit assessment is, by its nature, complex and fluid.
While some broad principles can be stated, the detailed real-time
decisions made by staff are not readily amenable to being documented.
The role of dynamic risk-benefit assessment may be undervalued by
risk assessment perspectives which focus on the need for written
evidence showing that procedures are being followed.

Risk–benefit assessment and current practice

Some providers may be wondering why they should move from their current risk management practice to the process of risk-benefit assessment recommended in this guide. It is only possible to be confident that play provision offers the best possible opportunities to children and young people if there is explicit consideration of the benefits. Play providers cannot demonstrate that they are meeting these objectives without such an assessment. It is therefore central to the task of providing play opportunities.

A growing number of providers, especially local authorities, have developed play policies and strategies. Many of these include statements about the value of play, making reference to risk and the need for a balanced approach. Some quote *Managing Risk in Play Provision*, either in part or in full, or endorse it in other ways. Such strategies and policies go some way towards the kind of policy framework required for risk-benefit assessment.

Few providers are currently using all levels of the risk–benefit management process.

Very few providers will currently be undertaking all four levels of risk-benefit management. Risk management as it is currently practiced is likely to include the following activities:

- procurement processes that require designs to be compliant with standards to a lesser or greater extent
- post-installation inspections by competent inspectors (in-house or external)
- annual inspections by competent inspectors (in-house or external)
- more frequent routine inspections by staff or volunteers.

Depending on the type of procurement processes and inspections being carried out, these activities may include an element of benefit assessment, perhaps expressed in terms of the play value of equipment or other aspects of the facility. They will therefore provide information relevant to both sides of the risk-benefit assessment.

Table 4 looks at two hypothetical providers – a local authority, and a parish council – to show how risk-benefit management might compare with current practice.

Table 4: Risk–benefit assessment in practice

Example: Local authority (LA) parks' manager with five parks and 100 play areas

Current regime	Risk-benefit management system
Weekly and quarterly inspections by sub-contracted company at existing play areas for wear and tear, litter hazards and damage.	Weekly and quarterly inspections by sub-contracted company at existing sites for wear and tear, litter hazards and damage.
Annual inspections at existing play areas, using externally defined procedures to assess compliance with standards. Some information on play value may also be generated.	Periodic risk-benefit assessment at existing play areas, defined for each site, using locally defined procedures to assess against LA play policy objectives to answer the question: 'How well do the sites provide the play opportunities our LA aims to offer, while managing the risks?'
Procurement/refurbishment of three play areas each year, using design and build from standards-compliant manufacturer. Post-installation inspection.	Procurement/refurbishment of three play areas each year, based on play policy objectives. Includes risk-benefit assessment by park manager of current practice on some key issues (see tables in Chapter 7). Post-installation inspection.
Ongoing management of park facilities, often involving reactive, ad-hoc responses to issues arising.	Ongoing management of park facilities, informed by periodic risk-benefit assessment.

Example: Parish Council with three play areas

Current regime	Risk–benefit management system
Weekly and quarterly inspections by Parish Council at existing sites for wear and tear, litter hazards and damage.	Weekly and quarterly inspections by Parish Council at existing sites for wear and tear, litter hazards and damage.
Annual inspections at existing sites against standard, using externally defined procedures to assess compliance with standard. Some information on play value may also be generated.	Annual risk–benefit assessment at existing sites against Parish Council's play policy objectives, using locally defined procedures to answer the question: 'How well do the sites provide the play opportunities our Parish Council aims to offer, while managing the risks?'
Procurement/refurbishment of one play area every 10 years, using design and build from standard-compliant manufacturer. Post-installation inspection.	Procurement/refurbishment of one play area every 10 years, based on Parish Council play policy objectives. Includes risk–benefit assessment by Parish Council of current practice on some key issues (see tables in Chapter 7). Post-installation inspection.

The role of common sense, experience and expertise

One of the merits of risk–benefit assessment is that it provides a framework for bringing to bear the common sense knowledge and experience that providers have acquired from a variety of sources, alongside expert advice and guidance. For instance, most adults are familiar with how children play on rocky areas of beaches or other naturally occurring rock formations. This accumulated wealth of experience is relevant when considering the inclusion of, for example, natural rock mounds and boulders in play provision or playable space, and it can readily be included as an element of a risk–benefit assessment.

Specialist inspectors can be a valuable source of advice and information, but the ultimate responsibility rests, by law, with the provider.

Also important in risk-benefit assessment is a degree of expert input, often from a play inspector. Providers need to be clear about the role and position of such experts, especially if they have been brought in from outside the organisation. Well trained inspectors and other experts with an understanding of children and play should be in a good position to give advice on technical issues that may be beyond the competence of providers, such as the content and implications of relevant material from industry standards. They may also be able to offer sound advice on other issues, such as: technical inspection of non-standard elements; how children play; the role and benefits of different play experiences and opportunities; and basic guidance on the law. However they are not in a position to take the responsibility for the final decisions about how best to strike the balance between risks and benefits in particular circumstances. They are a legitimate source of advice and information but the ultimate responsibility rests, by law, with the provider as duty-holder.

The Climbing Forest at Coombe Abbey Country Park does not conform neatly with EN1176 guidance. However, with correct use of risk assessment guided by EN1176 and thorough traversing/ testing of the equipment by an experienced inspector it was found to be acceptable. (Shackell A, 2008)

Photo: Aileen Shackell

If the provider and inspector do not agree about a judgement, the provider may wish to seek further advice.

Experts may also disagree on some issues. Where the views of the provider are at odds with those of the expert, providers should question the advice they receive. Providers may wish to seek further advice, though ultimately it is for them to weigh up the issues and make a judgement.

The following set of questions may help providers to get the best value from independent expert advice.

- Is the person a member of a recognised body, such as RPII, which ensures a minimum level of knowledge, competences and experience?

- Is the person clear about the role and advisory status of the standard?

- What competence does the person have in technical inspection of non-standard play features?

- What level of understanding does the person have about children's play?

- Has the person knowledge and expertise on play opportunities and equipment for disabled children?

- Is the person clear about their role in risk management – in particular that their job is to provide information and advice, and not to make final decisions?

- Has a clear brief been drawn up for the person about their role and the issues they should be addressing?

- Is the person's perspective on benefits and risks compatible with that of the provider?

- Can the person provide references to give assurances about the standard of their work?

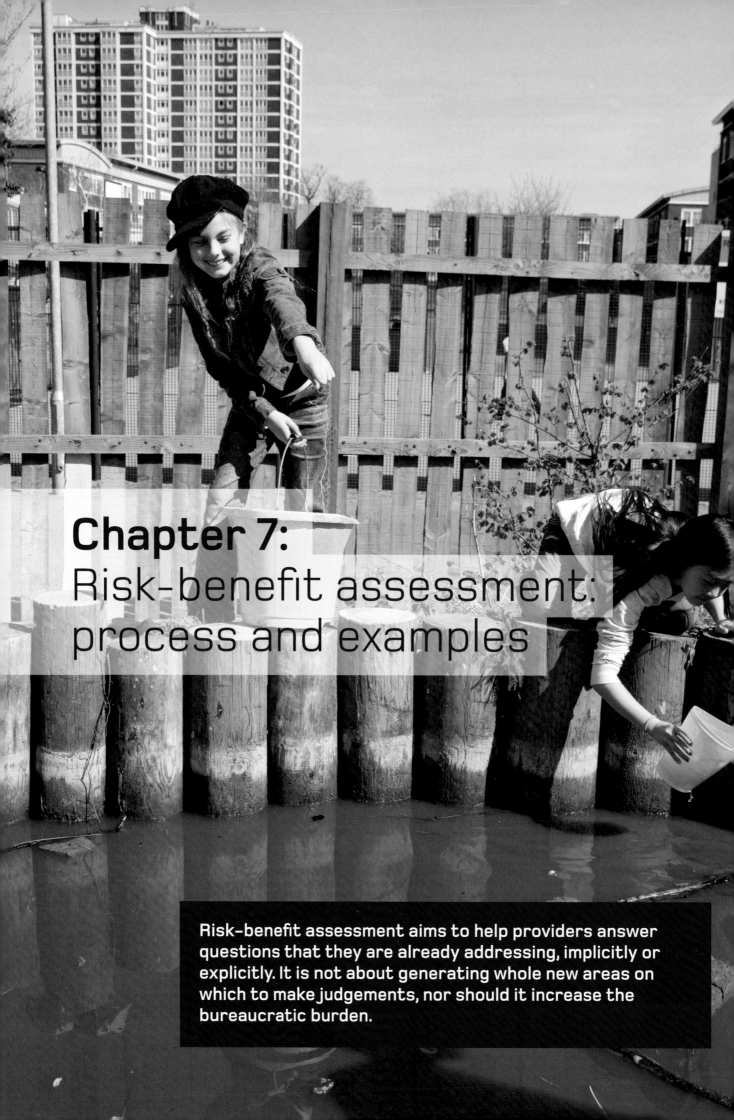

Chapter 7:
Risk-benefit assessment: process and examples

Risk-benefit assessment aims to help providers answer questions that they are already addressing, implicitly or explicitly. It is not about generating whole new areas on which to make judgements, nor should it increase the bureaucratic burden.

This chapter describes risk-benefit assessment in more detail and proposes a set of generic questions that can be used in assessing risks and benefits.

To illustrate the approach, this section discusses how risk-benefit assessment might be used in a variety of different situations.

Some of these topics are explored in detail. However, no final judgement is offered, because this will be dependent upon the values, policies and objectives of the provider, and on local circumstances.

This chapter describes in more detail the approach of risk-benefit assessment, which can only be carried out for a facility or space once the policy framework has been agreed by the organisation. This policy will underpin and inform all subsequent decisions about the nature and extent of play opportunities to be offered in a variety of different settings and situations.

Risk-benefit assessment highlights the balance of risks and benefits, and takes into account possible effects and side effects of the actions taken.

Risk-benefit assessment is a descriptive process which highlights the balance of risks and benefits in the light of a provider's play policy. It involves consideration of risks, benefits, and the possible effects and side-effects of measures proposed as a result. It needs to take into account local circumstances. It should allow for learning and sharing of approaches from other, comparable provision and from other relevant contexts.

Because children's play is an unpredictable, complex process, providers need to keep abreast of current practice and learn from other people's experiences.

In practice, the experience of others (both successful and unsuccessful) is amongst the most important source of good ideas and learning. Because children's play is an unpredictable, complex process, providers need to keep abreast of current practice and learn from other people's experiences. For example, providers who are considering whether or not to use dog-proof fencing, can learn from the experiences of others who have already taken this step.

As debate around risk and play becomes more accepting of the value of offering children and young people opportunities for risk and challenge, providers and designers are increasingly creating adventurous, engaging play environments that may not have been provided a few years ago. The signs are that this trend is growing.

Risk-benefit assessment supports these developments by offering a framework for challenge risk aversion.

However, there is still much room for improvement. For example, there is a sense that equipment in much play provision is designed to be 'safe' for young children, and may not be sufficiently challenging for older children and young people. If this is the case, it could be that the risk-taking needs of older children have been neglected. Historically, some authorities have been reluctant to provide skate parks and similar facilities. These higher-risk facilities have sometimes been resisted by safety officers. The situation has improved recently, in part, because new standards have been developed (BSI, 2006).

Providers and designers are increasingly creating adventurous, engaging play environments that may not have been provided a few years ago.

Photo: Play England/ Paul Upward

Risk–benefit assessment builds on current practice, and is not about adding bureaucracy.

Risk-benefit assessment is about building on current practice, not about generating unnecessary new areas for judgements, or increasing the bureaucratic burden. The process should be useful in addressing a wide range of topics and questions where risks and benefits are central considerations. Some examples include:

- different stages in the procurement process
- choices about the type and nature of play features or equipment to be included
- the use of fencing
- inclusion of non-prescriptive play features such as landscape features, logs, boulders and walls
- the use of impact attenuating surfacing (IAS)
- the inclusion of play equipment that does not comply with the relevant standard.

Risk-benefit assessment also has a role in the provision of playable spaces, such as parks, civic spaces, home zones or nature areas, for example it might be applied to:

- self-built structures such as dens, shelters, rope swings and tree houses
- design and management of playful landscape elements such as water features or public art
- features such as open water, buildings, architectural remains, or geological formations
- guidance on how staff intervene in children's and young people's behaviour.

The risk-benefit assessment process

Risk-benefit assessment allows the provider to arrive at an informed judgement, based on detailed consideration of the variety of issues relevant local circumstances. A descriptive record is kept throughout the process. This provides transparency and allows the provider to demonstrate the rationale behind all decisions about risk and safety.

The process uses a set of generic questions to assess the risks and benefits in relation to specific features in the playable space. The answers to these questions make up the descriptive risk-benefit assessment (see Table 5).

Table 5: Risk–benefit assessment: model questions

Questions for consideration	Possible sources of information
What are the benefits – for children and young people, and for others? What are the risks? What views are there on the nature of the risk, and how authoritative are they? What relevant local factors need to be considered? ● characteristics of the site ● local population and likely users ● other play opportunities nearby What are the options for managing the risk, and what are the pros, cons and costs of each? ● increase the opportunities for engagement (with good risk) ● do nothing ● monitor the situation ● mitigate or manage the risk ● remove the risk. What precedents and comparisons are there ● from other providers? ● from comparable places, spaces, services and activities? What is the risk-benefit judgement? How should the judgement be implemented in the light of local political concerns, cultural attitudes and beliefs?	These will vary depending on the topic under consideration. They could include: ● common sense, experience ● observation of play space/ equipment in use by children ● standards ● guidance and resources from relevant agencies ● expert opinion ● views of colleagues and peers ● relevant experience from other providers ● national data sources ● local data sources ● research studies ● local knowledge

The questions are a set of prompts, not a rigid list, and may need to be adapted to suit different situations. The precise questions, and format for addressing them, will be determined by the framework described in the organisation's play policy and agreed by the management.

For many people explicitly addressing the questions and recording the answers may simply be a more systematic way of capturing the information providers are already taking into account, and that is covered by standards, guidance and conventional risk assessment.

Tables 7 to 13 later in this chapter illustrate how the system might be used in some of these situations by offering theoretical answers to the model questions. They give examples of the nature of the descriptive assessment, but not the detail, as this will be dependent on local circumstances.

Providers should use their understanding of children's play needs, the need to offer risk and challenge and their own knowledge and experience to inform their judgements.

Providers, local circumstances and approaches to provision vary widely, so each risk-benefit assessment will be different; informed by the play policy framework, management perspectives and individual situation. As well as considering the law, standards and guidance, providers should use their understanding of children's play needs, the need to offer risk and challenge in play provision and their own knowledge and experience, whilst bearing in mind the advice of the HSE in *Five Steps to Risk Assessment* to 'focus on the risks that really matter' (HSE, 2006).

Risk–benefit assessment: an example

This fictitious case study shows how risk-benefit assessment might work in practice.

Townchester City Council is a densely populated urban area with limited green space. The council has adopted a play policy that recognises the value of managed risk-taking by children and young people, of contact with nature and natural environments, and of the health and welfare benefits of outdoor play.

The city council's parks manager wants children to have the chance to climb trees. However, some colleagues and elected members want to prohibit tree climbing because of fears of injury and possible litigation. The question being raised is about the general approach to tree-climbing across the authority, not the risks and benefits in relation to a specific tree or park. Table 6 shows the risk-benefit assessment, using the model questions. In this hypothetical example, the questions are answered and a judgement is offered which takes into account Townchester City Council's policy.

Table 6: Hypothetical risk–benefit assessment: should tree-climbing in Townchester's parks be allowed or prohibited?

Issue	Commentary	Information sources
Benefits	The pleasure it gives children and young people. Benefits to health, confidence and well-being. Benefits of regular contact with nature in promoting environmental awareness.	Forestry Commission *Growing Adventure* report (Gill, 2006). Play England publications on the benefits of play. Everyday experience and observation.
Risks	Risk of minor injuries and long bone fractures. Lesser risk of more serious injuries. Risk of damage to trees. Risk of complaints from some residents; risk of claims, litigation and loss of reputation.	National accident data. Local knowledge about injuries and complaint levels. Information about claims from colleagues and professional networks.
Expert views	Arboricultural inspection shows some obviously weak branches in some trees. Different expert views: positive attitudes from child development experts. Concerns from accident prevention professionals.	Arboricultural inspection reports. Play inspectors' views. Play England publications. Published guidance from accident prevention organisations.
Relevant local factors	Likely prevalence of tree-climbing. Location and species of trees.	Park managers.
Options and their costs, pros and cons	1. Leave trees as they are, and allow climbing. 2. Remove some weaker branches and allow climbing. 3. Remove trees and/or lower branches to prevent climbing. 4. Try to stop children from climbing by using enforcement and education. 5. Talk with children about making their own judgements about strength and safety of branches.	No new information: options need to be discussed and pros and cons weighed up.

Issue	Commentary	Information sources
	Arboricultural, educational or enforcement action all have financial costs. Removing weaker branches may send too strong a signal that the trees have been modified to make them safe for intensive climbing, and may encourage concentrated use. Enforcement is likely to antagonise children and be only partially successful. It may also lead children to go to elsewhere to climb, or do other less desirable things.	
Precedents/ comparisons	Cityville Metropolitan Borough Council has a policy allowing tree climbing and this has had a positive outcome.	Professional networks. Play England, Greenspace, CABE and other national agencies.
Risk–benefit judgement	In general benefits outweigh risks but these need to be managed, so leave trees as they are, and allow tree climbing. Monitor carefully at different times of year and review decision in one year or earlier if change in situation. Provide information to park staff and local people about decision and rationale.	
Implementing judgement locally	Tree-climbing as a child was a common experience for many adults, and something that many would agree is of value for children today. Parents, carers and other adults in a supervisory role are likely to set rules about tree-climbing, since they are aware of the risks. Consider publicising the decision, to demonstrate the city council's approach to risk-taking and to highlight this to parents.	Experience from others in similar circumstances, gained from professional networks. Support from national agencies.

[Note: in this example all statements are hypothetical.]

Illustration of risk–benefit assessment applied to specific issues

The examples described here offer ideas on how some specific topic areas can be examined using the descriptive approach to risk–benefit assessment in order to reach balanced judgements.

The topics and assessments are neither prescriptive nor exhaustive. Some providers may decide they do not need to address any of the topics explored below. Other providers may identify different topics that they feel would benefit from a risk-benefit assessment.

In each topic area, no final judgement is offered, because this will be dependent on the values, policies and objectives of the provider, and on local circumstances.

The following pages illustrate how risk–benefit assessment might be used in relation to:

- boundaries and fencing
- impact attenuating surfacing
- non-compliant fixed equipment
- self-build structures
- 'non-prescriptive' play features
- dogs and cats.

Boundaries and fences

In the UK – though not in some other European countries – it is common for play provision to be completely enclosed by fencing designed to prevent dogs from entering or leaving. This is the case whether or not dogs are seen as a problem. Apart from dog exclusion, the fencing is intended to make it more difficult for younger children to leave the play space and wander off.

Table 7 shows how risk-benefit assessment would address this question. In carrying out the assessment, providers would need to take into account the location of the provision in relation to roads, dog-walking areas, and any nearby hazards.

Case study:

Thurrock Council

Andy Furze, former green space manager of Thurrock Council, has described how his authority changed its approach to fencing.

'In Thurrock, all the play areas renewed in 1990 had been provided with a wood or metal fence around the equipment; in most cases the local "vandals" very sensibly and very quickly demolished and removed the fences; where they did remain we found they made little difference to levels of dog fouling anyway. Rather than spend further money on fencing, we found that the lack of fences enabled us to more easily expand areas, and allow children to freely move between equipment and the surrounding environment; on several sites we installed some simple mounds and copses of young trees, and it was good to find that once these became tall enough for children to hide in they were clearly being used by children. Our best play areas did not have fences!'
(Furze, 2006)

The absence of boundary fencing at Dilkes Park in Thurrock, gives the play area an informal quality, helping the play area to blur into the surrounding parkland.

Photo: Andy Furze

Table 7: Should fencing and boundaries be installed around this play provision?

Issue	Commentary	Information sources
Benefits of not having fencing around play areas	Children learn to regulate their exploratory play for themselves. Parents who come with their children pay more attention to where their children are, rather than assuming they cannot escape. Children can spread out in their play rather than having to remain in a confined space. In some locations, fencing can make dog problems worse: some dog-owners actively seek out fenced spaces to train and manage their dogs. Gates do not always close completely, making them ineffective at excluding dogs. Removes a potential hazard (children trying to climb fences, or simply using gates, can injure themselves). Reduced risk of the play area layout fostering bullying, harassment, victimisation or territorial behaviour. Allows alternative use of capital funds.	Play England publications on the benefits of play including *Design for Play* (Shackell A, and others, 2008). Everyday experience and observation.
Risks of having play areas with no fencing	Risk of harm from children leaving the area and encountering hazards beyond it, such as roads or open water. Potential for children to wander off and get lost. Fencing may help with dog management. Some children with specific learning difficulties or behavioural problems may be more difficult to supervise in unfenced provision.	Everyday experience and observation. Experience of carers of children with relevant impairments.
Expert views	Range of views, though a growing perspective amongst national agencies, designers and manufacturers that fencing is unnecessary in many circumstances.	Play inspectors; national play agencies.
Relevant local factors	Site-specific factors relating to hazards.	

Issue	Commentary	Information sources
Options and their pros and cons	Various options, ranging from fencing and other ways of defining boundaries to completely unfenced spaces. Pros and cons will depend on resources and site location.	No new information: options need to be discussed, or pros and cons weighed up.
Precedents/ comparisons	Thurrock and Stirling have avoided use of fencing. Mayor of London's planning guidance on play and informal recreation states that fencing should only be used where justified by the presence of hazards beyond the play space. Beaches: the way parents oversee their children on beaches shows that people feel comfortable in unfenced spaces, even if there are significant hazards nearby. Experiences of other agencies, such as nurseries and Forest Schools, may be valuable.	Play England design guide *Design for Play* (Shackell, A, and others, 2008). Fields in Trust forthcoming publication (*Planning and Design for Outdoor Sport and Play*). Mayor of London's supplementary planning guidance (GLA, 2008).
Risk–benefit judgement	Dependent on the values, policies and objectives of the provider, and on local circumstances.	
Implementing judgement locally	In some areas parents may be keen or even insistent on fencing. Some providers have successfully allayed concerns.	Experience in Thurrock and Stirling.

Impact attenuating surfacing

During the past 25 years, playgrounds in Britain have increasingly been fitted with impact attenuating surfacing (IAS) in the belief that this will reduce the severity of injuries from falls, especially head injuries. This development was in response to consumer safety lobby that developed in the late 1960s and early 1970s. The 2008 version of BS EN 1176 recommends IAS for fall heights greater than 0.6 metres, and in the UK, well-maintained grass is appropriate for fall heights of up to 1.5 metres, subject to a risk assessment (BSI, 2008a).

According to the Association of Play Industries (API), some types of IAS (particularly synthetic rubber bound with resin) can consume up to 40 per cent of capital budgets for conventional play provision. Although the primary objective of providing IAS is to afford some protection to users who may be engaged in potentially risky play activities many types in themselves do also provide opportunities for play. Different types of surface will have different capital and maintenance costs and offer different types of play value. The effectiveness of various forms of IAS as a safety measure has been investigated by the research community (Ball, 2002; Ball, 2004; Norton et al, 2004;Towner et al, 2001; Khambalia et al, 2006). Although BS EN 1176 has published the current majority European view, there are many other positions on this issue, some of which question whether it is 'reasonable' to recommend that IAS be used in all cases. Research continues into this issue.

Table 8 sets out how a risk–benefit assessment could address the selection of surface type in a particular location. It does not, however, attempt to address all the factors that might shape a final decision, such as the capital and maintenance costs of specific types of surfacing.

The primary objective of providing IAS (in this case sand) is to afford some protection to users who may be engaged in potentially risky play activities.

Photo: Play England

Table 8: What surfaces are needed in this play provision?

Issue	Commentary	Information sources
Benefits of different types of ground surface	Existing natural ground cover may be suitable for all or part of the play area and fit the surroundings and offer good play value. Natural surfaces are liked for their feel and play value. Some surfaces with lower capital costs will free up budget, which can be allocated to more equipment and other features with greater play value, and/or to ongoing maintenance. Surfaces that are not specifically designed to attenuate impacts are readily available and low cost, such as grass, sand or bark. It is reasonable to assume that the behaviour of children and their parents/carers may be modified by the type of surface provided (children may take more care over harder surfaces, and parents/carers may supervise younger children more closely). Children who do fall may learn valuable lessons about the consequences of falling on different kinds of surfaces that they will encounter in the wider world. There is uncertainty about the relative merits of different types of surface. Some biomechanical research suggests that some popular types of IAS (for example rubberised surfacing) may increase the likelihood of certain types of injuries, such as long-bone fractures. Likewise other types (for example loose fill) may reduce it.	Everyday observation. Research studies on IAS. Recommendations on safety policy by regulatory agencies. Analysis of previous provision.
Risks associated with different types of ground surface	Some biomechanical studies suggest that a lack of IAS type surfaces may increase the likelihood of certain types of injuries, such as head injuries although overall, the evidence is inconclusive. High cost surfaces will reduce available funds for other play provision. Insurers and the courts currently seem to expect that IAS will be fitted. Grass/topsoil may not be suitable in some situations where it will be eroded, such as under dynamic equipment.	Independent experts.

Issue	Commentary	Information sources
Expert views	European expert views are represented by majority in BS EN 1176, although there are differing opinions. Safety and accident prevention experts tend to favour IAS as a reasonable safety precaution. There has been a challenge to the case for IAS in general and to whether it is consistent with the principle of reasonable practicability.	BS EN 1176 (BSI, 2008a). Research studies on IAS and public policy on safety. Independent experts.
Relevant local factors	The design of the space, including the equipment and other features to be included. The users (age, numbers etc) of the equipment and their expectations. Type of play activity and any structures being provided.	
Options and their pros and cons	Decide on key requirements a) Does IAS need to be provided? b) Does the whole area need the same type of surfacing? c) Type of surface preferred in different locations. The final decision will also be influenced by other considerations, such as capital and maintenance costs, alternative uses of funds, play value, aesthetics, suitability for site, flammability.	No new information: options need to be discussed and pros and cons weighed up.
Precedents/ comparisons	The 2008 version of BS EN 1176 has redefined its recommendations on the need for certain types of IAS in recognition of the need for a balance between cost, risk and benefit.	BS EN 1176
Risk-benefit judgement	Dependent on the values, policies and objectives of the provider, and on local circumstances.	
Implementing judgement locally	The choice of surfacing, whether the existing ground surface, or one or more of the many types of IAS requires careful planning and consultation, and possible promotion of the benefits of the selected surface.	

Non-compliant fixed equipment

Some play equipment manufacturers are willing, and have the experience, to supply play equipment that is not covered by or does not conform to industry standards. This is because some providers may wish to offer play opportunities that are difficult or impossible to realise within the parameters of the standard. Although such equipment is not compliant with the standard, it is still possible to use it, as long as a suitable and sufficient risk-benefit assessment has been carried out. Manufacturers who provide such non-compliant equipment should, where appropriate, provide documented technical data, to be included in the provider's risk-benefit assessment.

Table 9 sets out how a risk-benefit assessment might address the use of equipment or features that do not comply with industry standards (non-compliant play equipment and features).

Table 9: Should this play equipment, that does not meet industry standards, be included in this play area?

Issue	Commentary	Information sources
Benefits of non-compliant play equipment	Benefits of offering play opportunities that may be difficult or impossible to achieve within the parameters of the standard.	Observation of children at play.
Risks	Unacceptable hazards or bad risks may be introduced through poor design or construction. Risk assessments and inspections may not be consistent compared to those carried out on standard equipment, and may be less reliable in court cases.	Professional experience. Play inspectors. Principles of BS EN 1176.
Expert views	Some play experts and playground inspectors recognise the value of using non-compliant equipment as long as a suitable inspection/ assessment has been carried out.	
Relevant local factors	The equipment being proposed, its location in relation to other equipment and features, and the characteristics of the wider area.	
Pros and cons of options	Options, and their pros and cons, will be site-specific. No data that injuries involving such features are more or less likely.	No new information. Options need to be discussed and pros and cons weighed up.

Issue	Commentary	Information sources
Precedents/ comparisons	Providers are increasingly using non-prescriptive play features. Stirling Council is one authority regularly doing this – see case study (page 88) and case study below.	Professional networks. Play England, Greenspace, CABE and other national agencies.
Risk-benefit judgement	Dependent on the values, policies and objectives of the provider, and on local circumstances.	
Implementing judgement locally	A small but growing minority of providers are willing to consider such an approach. Parents with preconceived ideas about play space may need to be persuaded of the merits of different approaches.	

Case study:

Cutsyke Play Forest, standards and the role of risk-benefit assessment

Cutsyke Play Forest

At Cutsyke, the highest platform intended for climbing is 4-metres above the ground.

Photo: Robin Sutcliffe

Case study:

Cutsyke Play Forest, standards and the role of risk-benefit assessment

The Cutsyke Play Forest, a play space in Castleford, West Yorkshire, incorporates a structure that does not adhere to the European Standard. A climbing feature within the play forest comprises a series of 6-metre poles, slides, netting and elevated, open platforms that are 4-metres above the ground. BS EN 1176 states that the maximum acceptable fall height should be 3-metres. Netting around most of the platforms, however, meant that fall heights to the nets, but not to the ground surface, are within the 3 metres limit and in the areas where there are no nets, 1.3-metre high barriers have been erected to reduce the likelihood of falls from 4-metres.

The play forest could not have been realised if the local authority, the community or the play design company had felt themselves unduly restricted by the requirements of BS EN 1176. It was recognised that the standard is not mandatory, thus creating scope for interpretation and variation within the wider context of risk-benefit assessment.

The play forest was independently inspected during the design process, and again on completion, for 'bad risks' – for example, checks were carried out for structural soundness and to ensure that there were no unexpected protuberances. These inspections were carried out with reference to BS EN 1176 to ensure that any deviations were fully understood. The wider context for the inspection was the understanding that the play forest would be of benefit to children, young people and the local community. This understanding, coupled with the inspector's judgement that the risk of falling was sufficiently mitigated by the netting and the barriers, resulted in a risk assessment which recommended that no further action was necessary.

Another interesting feature of the play forest scheme was the attitude of the local community and the commissioning authority to the winning design. Any concerns they may have had about the structure were allayed. This suggests that it is a mistake to assume that community or public opinion will automatically be risk-averse and unable to appreciate the wider benefits of risk-taking in play.

Self-built structures

Structures such as dens, rope swings and tree houses have been built by children for generations, and are still found in many public spaces, woodlands and parks today. However, they also raise safety issues, especially in designated play areas where children and parents may have higher expectations about the strength or soundness of structures and where the numbers of children using them is likely to increase the potential for wear and tear.

Table 10 sets out how a risk-benefit assessment would address issues raised by the presence of children and young people's self-built structures. It is intended for use in unsupervised play areas. The issues will be different in staffed play provision, such as adventure playgrounds or where play rangers are present.

Table 10: What approach should be taken to the presence of children and young people's self-built structures?

Issue	Commentary	Information sources
Benefits of allowing self-built structures	Children greatly enjoy building, using and modifying structures. Such structures signify a strong sense of ownership by children. Their presence can enrich play spaces and make them locally distinctive, at little or no cost.	Numerous studies on children's outdoor play. Everyday experience and observation.
Risks	Built structures may present some bad risks. Their location may increase risks of falls. Rope swings may break unexpectedly, they have a risk of strangulation, and they may be located near or above hazardous objects. Structures may encourage inappropriate behaviour, or generate litter or food debris. Concentrated use may add wear and tear.	Everyday experience and observation. Experience of play inspectors. Principles of BS EN 1176.
Expert views	Play and child development experts assert the developmental value of self-built structures. Concerns from safety experts about the presence of self-built structures in dedicated play provision.	
Relevant local factors	The nature and types of self-built structure present, their locations and levels of use. Where self-built structures are located within play areas, parents and children may have higher expectations of their structural soundness.	

Issue	Commentary	Information sources
Options and their pros and cons	1. Remove/destroy structures. 2. Modify structures (with or without input from children). 3. Leave structures alone. 4. Attempt to create comparable play experiences in a different way. 5. Allow self-built structures only in staffed provision. Removal of structures will upset and potentially alienate users. Modification with children's input could be time-consuming, but may encourage them to take a more responsible approach. The merits of different approaches will be highly dependent on location of structure.	No new information: options need to be discussed and pros and cons weighed up.
Precedents/ comparisons	Some park managers routinely remove self-built structures, especially from play areas. The Royal Parks allow dens to be built in Richmond Park. The Forestry Commission has published guidance on managing risks relating to self-built structures in its own woodlands, although this guidance is not intended for application to public play areas. Other guidance specifically for adventure playgrounds also exists.	Forestry Commission guidance *Rope Swings, Dens, Tree Houses and Fires: A risk based approach for managers facilitating self-built play structures and activities* (Harrop, 2006). This applies to Forestry Commission land specifically. *Risk and Safety in Play* (PLAYLINK, 1997).
Risk–benefit judgement	Dependent on the values, policies and objectives of the provider, and on local circumstances.	
Implementing judgement locally	Local attitudes may vary widely: in some areas there may be some hostility, in others there may be a longstanding local tradition of structure building.	

'Non-prescriptive' play features

Many providers restrict their provision to equipment that has been pre-assessed against industry standards and found to meet them. While this may offer providers reassurance, it can lead them to ignore non-prescriptive play elements or features such as logs, boulders, hard landscaping, planting or changes of level. Although these features are not specifically covered by industry standards they can still be included in playable spaces, provided they have been tested with a suitable risk-benefit assessment. These features can add to the play offer and may broaden the range of benefits to users.

Case study:

The Forestry Commission

The Forestry Commission has published design guidance for its staff on creating natural play spaces that complement woodland settings. The guidance discusses landform, vegetation management, natural features, water and mud, and safety surfacing, amongst other issues. It states that the aim is 'to create naturalistic play spaces that act as a springboard for children's engagement with forests and woodlands as a whole. They should encourage children to explore the natural environment and to take part in active play where they have the opportunity to create their own play environments and activities.'
Design guidance for play spaces
(Houston, Worthington and Harrop, 2006)

Playing on the woodpecker play sculpture in Alice Holt Woodland Park.

Photo: Forestry Commission/Isobel Cameron

Table 11 sets out how risk-benefit assessment might address the use of non-prescriptive play features such as logs, boulders, hard landscaping, planting or changes of level.

Table 11: Should natural features and landscaping be included in this play area?

Issue	Commentary	Information sources
Benefits of non-prescriptive play features	Benefits of contact with natural materials and plants in engaging children and enriching their play. Benefits in promoting environmental awareness. Can be a low-cost way to provide different play opportunities and improve design.	Everyday experience. Observation of children at play. Experience of providers using this approach.
Risks	Unacceptable hazards or bad risks may be introduced through poor design or construction. Risk assessments and inspections do not have a readily available benchmark.	Professional experience. Play inspectors.
Expert views	Some play experts promote the benefits of natural play environments.	Play England publication: *Play, Naturally* (Lester, S and Maudsley, M, 2006).
Relevant local factors	The features being proposed, their location in relation to equipment and other features, the characteristics of the site, and the accessibility and quality of natural environments nearby.	
Pros and cons of options	Options, and their pros and cons, will be site-specific. No data that injuries involving such features are more or less likely.	No new information: options need to be discussed and pros and cons weighed up.
Precedents/comparisons	Stirling Council makes extensive use of non-prescriptive play features – (see case study page 88). Most adults have experience of climbing on rocks and playing in woods and natural areas, and experience of watching children in these contexts. Articulating this experience will help inform the judgement.	Professional networks. Play England, Greenspace, CABE and other national agencies.
Risk-benefit judgement	Dependent on the values, policies and objectives of the provider, and on local circumstances.	
Implementing judgement locally	A small but growing number of providers are willing to consider such an approach. Parents with preconceived ideas about play space may need to be persuaded of the merits of different approaches.	

Dogs and cats

There is potential for conflict in many types of public space over use between dogs (and dog owners) and children. However, many people are both parents and dog owners, and some spaces are successfully shared by dogs and children. A risk-benefit assessment can help providers to make judgements about how best to manage these issues.

Table 12 sets out how a risk-benefit assessment would address the issue of dog management. The assessment would need to take into account local circumstances such as patterns of use (by dog owners and children), attitudes and behaviour of dog owners and the physical nature of the space.

The health risks associated with cats in play provision are similar but less severe than with dogs. In both cases the main risk is from toxocariasis, and tends to be restricted to play areas with loose earth and loose fill materials, especially sand and gravel. With cats the risk is low since they rarely cross large expanses of open ground when looking for places to defaecate.

Table 12: Should dogs and cats be restricted from entering/using this area where children play?

Issue	Commentary	Information sources
Benefits of allowing contact with dogs	Some children like dogs and cats. Allowing interaction with dogs may enable children to become more confident about dealing with dogs. Indirect benefits if dog-proof fencing is avoided, since this allows scope for more flexible designs, and more flexible use of public open space (see Table 7 above).	Everyday experience and observation. Play England's design guidance *Design for Play* (Shackell, A and others, 2008).
Risks	Some children are afraid of dogs. Risk of attack. Risk of toxocariasis from ingesting faecal material. The risk from toxocariasis is small and has been getting smaller over the years. Toxocariasis is fairly common but most cases result in a complete recovery. However, around 50 people a year suffer permanent eye damage, nearly all as a result of infection during early childhood. Around 1,600 children each year attend A&E as a result of a dog bite. It is unclear how many cases of toxocariasis or dog bites arise from play provision.	Encams website www.encams.org.

Issue	Commentary	Information sources
Expert views	There are a range of views on how to address the issue.	Play inspectors. RoSPA. Dog wardens.
Relevant local factors	Levels of dog ownership; behaviour of dog owners; scope for education and enforcement initiatives.	
Options and their pros and cons	1. Dog-proof fencing. 2. Creating barriers and boundaries in other ways. 3. Education and enforcement. 4. Dog bans. 5. Signage and water supply for hand washing. Fencing can cost 10 per cent of total capital costs of a play area. It can lead to increased bullying and territorialism. It may also fail to solve the problem: some dog owners take their dogs into fenced play areas because it stops them running off. Education and enforcement have been effective in some local authorities in promoting responsible dog ownership. Dog bans are difficult to enforce and may be excessive (or perceived to be so). Signage and water supplies have rarely been adopted as a solution, but may work in locations where such facilities are being considered for other reasons.	No new information: options need to be discussed and pros and cons weighed up.
Precedents/ comparisons	Some local authorities report rising levels of responsible behaviour by dog owners supervising and cleaning up after their dogs. Thurrock and Stirling Councils (see case studies on pages 73 and 88) have rejected fencing as a solution. Each has successfully encouraged responsible dog ownership and shared use of play space.	Case studies in this guide. Professional networks. Play England, Greenspace, CABE and other national agencies.
Risk-benefit judgement	Dependent on the values, policies and objectives of the provider, and on local circumstances.	
Implementing judgement locally	The culture and attitudes of parents and dog-owners can vary widely in different locations.	

Case study:

Stirling Council

Stirling Council's play provision aims to create natural environments for play in a variety of settings: rural, semi-rural and urban. They are equally committed to creating play places that evoke a 'sense of place', such that each play area is unique to its particular setting.

Stirling play service has long taken the view that places for play do not necessarily need to be fenced, that rubber IAS has little or no play value and is not cost effective in terms of its potential to yield benefit, and that grass, water, sand, grit and natural features generally are key components of a quality play environment.

Stirling's approach to fencing, IAS, paddling pools and the use of sand runs counter to conventional opinion and this might be thought to be a source of difficulty, if not conflict, with parents in particular. In fact, partly as a result of Stirling's play services' commitment to explaining and demonstrating the benefits of their approach, initial anxieties have been allayed.

Stirling Council

At Causeway Park the play spaces were opened up to the surrounding park by removing fencing. The paddling pool was revitalised by the addition of decked platforms.

Photo: Stirling Council
Play Services

Thus, new schemes will generally not be fenced yet will feature sand or grit because of their inherent play potential, and sometimes also because of their impact absorbing qualities. Not unusually, parents' initial reaction is to be concerned about the potential for dog mess, and in any case to favour rubber impact absorbing surfacing because it is thought to be 'safer'.

However, after discussion, and as the result of seeing images of children and young people playing in sand and grit, people change their minds and recognise the value of using natural, environmentally friendly, manipulable materials. The result is that for over 10 years rubber IAS has not been used. There are no records of parental complaint or legal claims in respect of these sites.

This suggests that there is significant scope for changing perceptions so long as play providers are clear and robust about their values and understandings, coupled with a commitment to honest engagement with local communities. This is different from simply asking people what they want in their local play area. It is a process of learning.

Stirling Council

At Causeway Head children enjoy channelling both sand and water – these two elements are vital components to play environments across Stirling.

Photo: Stirling Council
Play Services

Other topics that might be subject to risk–benefit assessment

Risk–benefit assessment is a tool for improving decision–making in any context where a balance has to be struck between risks and benefits. In addition to the topics covered above, the approach could also be applied to the following issues:

● procurement processes (these may contain requirements that work against striking a good balance between risks and benefits)

● water features such as ponds, lakes, river and canal banks and streams

● fire pits, in both play provision and other playable spaces.

While the topics mentioned so far focus largely on physical risks, the same approach can be taken to social and other risks. For instance, some local authorities have a policy of removing hedges, enclosed structures and seating from play areas, because of the social risks they are thought to introduce. The justification given for this may be that it protects children against strangers, or that it dissuades others from using the play space for inappropriate purposes. Whatever the justification, risk–benefit assessment should help in reviewing such policies.

Risk–benefit assessment can be used to strike a balance between the risks and benefits of including water features such as this pond at Somerford Grove Adventure Playground.

Photo: Play England/ Philip Wolmuth

Setting priorities in risk management

A central element of risk management is setting priorities for mitigating existing unacceptable risks.

Some local authorities and housing associations, for example, have a large portfolio of play areas. Their provision may include old equipment that is in a poor state of repair. In these circumstances it is important to have in place risk management procedures that set priorities in a consistent and reliable way. Experienced, independent inspectors should be able to offer advice and support on this.

Chapter 8:
Developing and underpinning practice

Developing existing risk management procedures to incorporate risk–benefit assessment will require a review which results in procedures that are locally determined by the provider, in the light of the provider's policy framework and objectives, and local circumstances. Consulting and involving local parents and carers in discussions about the organisation's policy on risk and challenge in play provision is important to ensure they understand the approach and decisions taken.

This chapter shows how providers can develop and consolidate the approach to risk management set out in previous chapters. The area that is most likely to be new to many providers is risk–benefit assessment. One way to begin this process is to carry out a systematic review of risk management activities. Alternatively, providers may wish to introduce risk–benefit assessment in stages.

This section discusses insurance, including suggestions about how insurance and claims management policies and procedures can help support a robust approach to risk–benefit assessment.

It also discusses monitoring, communications and what to do if things go wrong.

Implementing risk–benefit assessment

Whilst technical inspection is common practice for most play providers and many have some kind of policy statement on risk, all providers, large and small, should develop an agreed statement on their approach to offering and managing opportunities for risk and challenge in play provision.

This might be part of an organisational play strategy or policy. In many areas play policies, both existing and new, may need to be reviewed to ensure they provide clear risk–benefit policy framework. For many organisations the process most likely to be new to them is the risk–benefit assessment process.

Local children, young people and parents should be encouraged to understand the approach to risk–benefit assessment.

Once a risk management policy for play provision has been agreed, the risk–benefit assessment process can be introduced in one of two ways. The first way is to carry out a systematic review of existing risk management activities, agreeing the revised process. Such a review might cover:

- procurement processes
- routine inspection, and training and support for this
- annual and post-installation inspections
- operational management (cleansing, grass-cutting, horticultural management)
- park warden/ranger services.

Alternatively, providers may wish to take a more reactive approach, introducing risk-benefit assessment as a revision of their existing regimens in a staged fashion, when relevant issues are under consideration. For example, a new procurement project could prompt risk-benefit assessment of aspects of a site brief, such as fencing and boundaries, landscape elements, IAS and equipment specification. Operational or organisational reviews may provide opportunities to develop risk-benefit assessment in other areas.

A new project could prompt risk-benefit assessment of fencing and boundaries, landscape elements, IAS and equipment specification.

Radnor Street Gardens in Islington uses 'non-prescriptive' play features such as boulders and gradients. Although not covered by standards they can be included if they have been subject to a suitable risk-benefit assessment.

Photo: Tim Gill

Insurance

The role of insurance is to provide a financial safety net for providers in the aftermath of accidents or other losses. It should never be the driver of risk management. Risk-benefit assessment, of the type recommended here, should assist both providers and insurers in containing the number of claims that are placed.

It is important that providers seek out insurance cover which meets their own specific needs. Public liability insurance is essential, and providers with staff are legally required to have employers' liability insurance. Insurance brokers can arrange cover, and well trained, experienced playground inspectors, who have a good understanding of children's play needs, may also be able to advise. Providers may find it useful to share experiences with each other.

Some local authorities and larger organisations are self-insured for claims up to a certain amount, giving more freedom to make judgements.

Providers should review their insurance arrangements regularly. Some local authorities and larger organisations have, in effect, self-insured for claims up to a certain amount, by raising their policy excesses. This gives them more freedom to judge each case on its merits. This option may not be open to smaller agencies that do not have the financial resources to cope with managing claims. However, even here there may be opportunities for agencies to come together under umbrella schemes to spread the financial risks.

Relatively few claims are made in respect of play provision, and there are even fewer instances of courts finding play providers negligent.

It is the provider's duty to ensure that its insurance arrangements support the implementation of its key play objectives. Although there is an inevitable tension between a play provider's goal of maximising public benefit, and the insurer's legitimate need to generate profit, these can be reconciled, as the experience of Wolverhampton City Council demonstrates (see case study below). In addition, both play providers and insurers need to be aware that relatively few claims are made in respect of play provision, and there are fewer cases still of courts finding play providers negligent. This should inform any discussion about premiums, levels of cover and any additional conditions.

Case study:

Wolverhampton City Council

Wolverhampton City Council's approach to risk and liability is based on two key principles: fairness and a policy-based commitment to maximise public benefit. Wolverhampton's risk management practice is founded on the understanding that there is a balance to be struck between risk and benefit, and that it is the council's duty to make judgements which advance the general public good.

Wolverhampton Council is predominantly self-insured in respect of its liability risks (it carries its own excess of £250,000). It is council policy to defend robustly any claim where it does not consider itself liable. It is also council policy to settle claims quickly where it judges that it has been at fault. In the words of the Risk and Insurance Manager, Wolverhampton City Council has developed a 'culture of defending claims but providing a firm but fair settlement in respect of those where it is liable'.

All claims are handled internally. Decision-making about how to respond to claims is delegated to the council's Risk and Insurance Manager, who works with an in-house claims team. Generally the council's insurers are not involved in the decision-making process, though they may be consulted in the event of a claim being made that could result in liabilities beyond the self-insured limit. However, this rarely occurs.

The Council, along with the voluntary sector, worked with PLAYLINK to develop a corporate, cross-sectoral play policy in the period 2005–06. The process of policy formation involved members, health and safety officers, parks, planners and the play department. Exploring attitudes to, and understandings about, risk in play formed an integral part of the process.

Wolverhampton's play policy, incorporating the Play Safety Forum's position statement, *Managing Risk in Play Provision*, was agreed by the council in 2007. The play policy slots neatly into Wolverhampton's general approach to risk management outlined above.

The council recognised that a play policy alone would not be sufficient to embed a culture change in the staff responsible for all forms of play provision. It was recognised that many of those involved in delivering play opportunities tended to 'go for safety', and that the 'fear factor' – about potential claims, and parental or other complaints – led to defensive practice.

As a result, the Risk and Insurance Manager and the Play Officer are creating a learning programme on risk and play for all staff whose decisions have an impact on play provision. This learning programme forms part of council's play strategy, and aims to create practitioners who are confident to make judgements about the risk-benefit balance in the range of situations they encounter.

Wolverhampton City Council

Right: ▶

Wolverhampton City Council's risk management practice is founded on striking a balance between risk and benefit.

Below left and Right: ▼▼

In the past those involved in delivering play opportunities tended 'to go for safety'. A learning programme has given practitioners the confidence to make decisions about risk–benefit judgements in a range of situations.

Photos: Wolverhampton City Council

The insurance market is subject to periodic fluctuations and trends that can have far-reaching effects on the market. For instance, premiums for public liability insurance increased sharply during the period 2002–03. While the causes are not agreed, one factor was the high cost to the insurance sector of meeting claims relating to such issues as asbestosis and other industrial hazards, natural disasters and terrorist attacks. In the following years, premiums did not rise as much, and some providers found that insurers were more open to flexible approaches, with signs of a more open market for policies..

Monitoring and audit trail

Keeping good records is part of any sound risk management system. As with risk assessment itself, common sense helps inform decisions about what needs to be recorded. As the HSE states, sensible risk management is not about 'generating useless paperwork mountains'. The most important thing to monitor is the overall performance of the provision, taking into account risks and benefits, in order to see if it is working as planned, or needs modification.

Close monitoring will show if any adjustment needs to be made to the assessment.

Photo: Play England

Risk–benefit assessments and technical inspections need to make reference to the policy framework.

The policy framework should be set out in a play policy. Risk-benefit and technical inspections need to be linked to this policy framework, and to make reference to it. Written risk-benefit assessments and technical inspections need to be kept in ways that allow them to be easily retrieved, and the system as whole should be designed to provide timely reminders for routine actions such as maintenance and inspections. Providers who have a large portfolio of play spaces may find it useful to use software packages and mobile technology. Commercial packages are available for this purpose, and experienced playground inspectors should be able to give advice.

Communications strategy

Providers should give clear information at all sites about who to contact if there are problems. Signage also provides an opportunity to convey to parents, carers and children messages about the provider's approach to risk management and safety.

The signage at play areas in Walsall urges children to play safely and provides contact information to report faulty items and give feedback.

Photo: Play England

For example, a sign might include the summary statement from the Play Safety Forum's *Managing Risk in Play Provision* [see page 112], to highlight the fact that the play space is designed with an element of risk, and that minor injuries in particular are to be expected. Such statements have little or no value in law and are not a defence against claims. Their point is to help raise awareness amongst parents and carers about the nature and role of play in children's lives and healthy development. It will be an added bonus if this reduces the number of inappropriate complaints and claims. Copies of the provider's play policy should be publicised and made available on request. Comments should always be considered and responded to.

Signage provides an opportunity to convey to parents, carers and children messages about the provider's approach to risk management and safety.

Providers may wish to make a public statement about their approach to managing risks, highlighting the fact that their provision aims to give children the chance to face real challenges with some risk of injury. Debates about the alleged overprotection of children and its impact on child development are matters of lively discussion in the media and more widely. Positive media coverage should help to get valuable messages across, both internally and to the public, about the need for a balanced approach.

What to do if things go wrong

Play provision is comparatively safe, and serious accidents of any kind are unlikely in the ordinary run of events. Nonetheless, they do happen from time to time. On these rare occasions, it is important to conduct a balanced and transparent review. It may be helpful to seek independent expertise about how this should be carried out.

Such a review must never attempt to hide possible poor, negligent or criminal behaviour on the part of the provider. Equally, it must also avoid knee-jerk responses to tragedy. There are genuine accidents, and the fact that a child has died or sustained a serious or permanent injury is not in itself proof that someone has done something wrong. Given the complex chain of events that precedes any incident, it is nearly always possible to find at least one point in the chain when, with the benefit of hindsight and in the knowledge of the ensuing tragedy, an action or omission might appear to be a negligent or culpable mistake (Adams, 1995). Reviews must always take proper account of the circumstances and issues that those taking the decisions and judgements were concerned about at the time.

PART 3

Concluding remarks

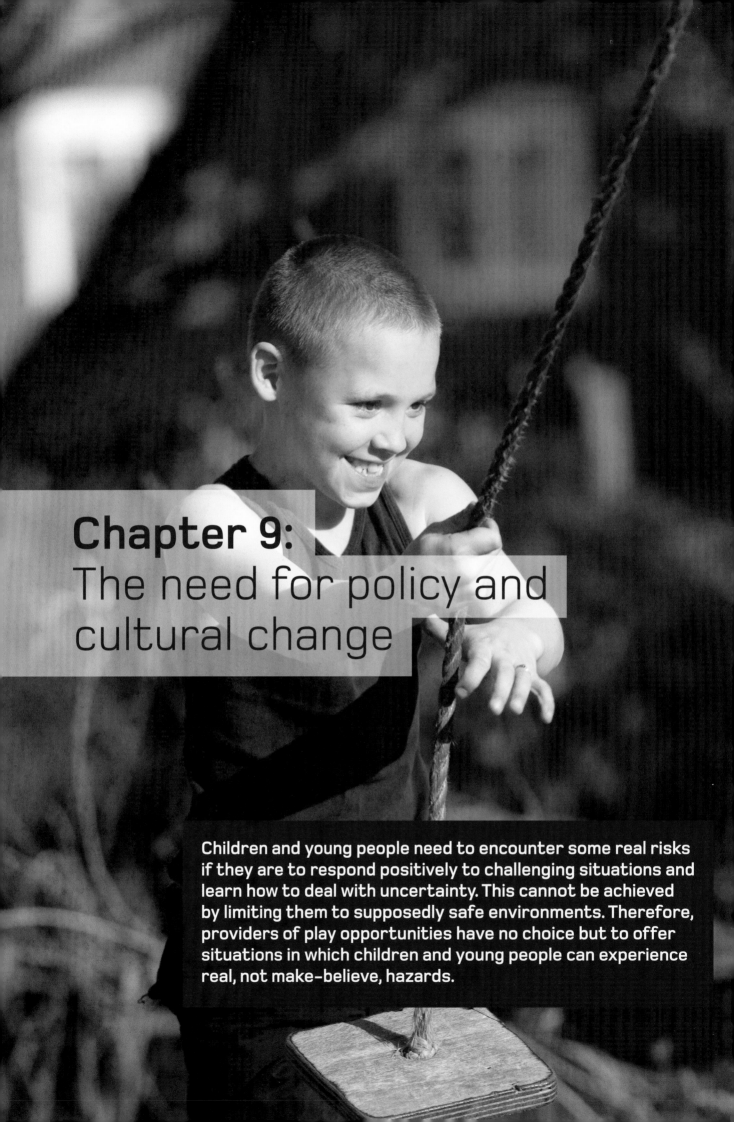

Chapter 9:
The need for policy and cultural change

Children and young people need to encounter some real risks if they are to respond positively to challenging situations and learn how to deal with uncertainty. This cannot be achieved by limiting them to supposedly safe environments. Therefore, providers of play opportunities have no choice but to offer situations in which children and young people can experience real, not make-believe, hazards.

This chapter discusses some current policy and cultural issues. These relate to: training and dissemination; natural play; evidence-based practice; the role of standards; the role of the Health and Safety at Work etc Act 1974; and the need for society as a whole to be more forgiving.

Discussion about risk and benefit in play provision should be continually reviewed.

The balance between avoiding risks of injury and experiencing the benefits of play needs to be continually reviewed as experiences and social expectations change. Recently, widespread and accumulating concerns about the state of childhood have signalled the need for a reappraisal. This process has already started and is now gathering pace and direction.

If we don't allow children to experience managed risk I have grave concerns about the future for workplace health and safety. If the next generation enter the workplace having been protected from all risk they will not be so much risk averse as completely risk naïve – creating an enormous task and dilemma for their employers – how to start that health and safety education process **or** to continue to try to protect them from all risk which is of course impractical and impossible.

(Judith Hackitt, Chair of the Health and Safety Executive)

The practical sections of this guide aim to help providers do a better job of balancing the benefits and risks of providing opportunities for children and young people's play, given the current legal, policy and cultural context. However, providers can only go so far, and there may also need to be some policy, practice and attitudinal changes if they are to succeed.

Practice development

If the approach to risk management proposed in this guide is to become widespread, a comprehensive programme of training and dissemination may be required. All those providing guidance and training to play providers are encouraged to review and, if appropriate, revise their materials and programmes. It may be that existing training programmes can be modified, although the need for additional support and new types of expertise cannot be ruled out. The benefits of play experiences, including to children's health and well-being, need proper emphasis, and appropriate expertise should be drawn from the relevant quarters.

In naturalistic play areas, risk management is less well developed and may need a different approach from that taken with conventional fixed equipment play areas.

One specific area of practice that has attracted attention is the trend towards creating more naturalistic play environments, with greater use of non-prescriptive play features such as logs, boulders, slopes, ditches and planting, along with sand and water. This trend is seen as desirable by most in the field. However, risk management of such forms of provision is not well developed, and existing standards are only partially relevant. Moreover, the highly variable style and features of such environments are not compatible with the kind of codification and normalisation that inevitably comes with the development of new standards. Such environments need a different approach from that taken with conventional fixed equipment play areas.

Another aspect of practice development that needs to be pursued is the need for a more evidence-based approach.

Standards compliance

As has been stated previously, compliance with standards is not mandatory. However, there is an undeniable difficulty here. Some institutions, courts, and insurance companies tend to use compliance with standards as the sole evidence of good practice. As a result, non-compliance may be used against duty holders as evidence of a failure to manage risk. This is a difficult situation, as it can foster an unadventurous approach which deters providers from experimenting with new types of provision.

The basis, role and purpose of standards all need to be much more widely understood. Standards incorporate difficult value judgements about what is an acceptable level of risk. With the possible exception of eliminating hazards such as head traps, standards do not pretend to eliminate risk. The implication is that standards are partly subjective and should be recognised as incorporating value-based judgements with a degree of uncertainty. Standards also need to be interpreted in the light of local circumstances. In many situations, standards should not be regarded as providing definitive answers, but should be seen as a guide to what is reasonable.

Public policy

Children's play provision, like other public spaces, is deemed to come under the Health and Safety at Work etc Act 1974. For those who work in these locations, the Act may well be appropriate, but some experts believe there are good reasons for thinking that, in this context, public risks may not be best served by the Health and Safety at Work etc Act. This is because the Act has come to be associated with a way of thinking and an approach to risk assessment that struggles with, and frequently omits, the consideration of benefits alongside risks..

Although it is less easy to measure the benefits of play provision than to measure physical injuries, the importance to the community of providing challenging play opportunities is now widely recognised and is increasingly backed by evidence.

An approach, which focuses on minimising risk, is also potentially damaging to the standing of risk management itself. There needs to be more public policy debate about how risks are managed in the public realm, and some respondents to the *Fair Play* consultation asked whether or not the Health and Safety at Work etc Act provides the right legal framework.

The 'border swing' at Slade Gardens Adventure Playground is a firm favourite with local children, even though everyone usually ends up on the ground: 'One person gets on, then everyone else jumps on you. You can get about six people on ...'

(PlayToday, 2008).

Photo: Play England

Attitudes to risk: a more forgiving society?

Ultimately, responsibility for play provision, or for a playable space, resides with the provider. Providers are now being urged to move the frontiers by being less risk averse, in order to reap the rewards for children and young people of a freer, more active and more natural lifestyle. When accidents happen, as is inevitable, providers may be called to account.

Providers may only be able to offer the new play opportunities that will challenge the current risk-averse culture by experimenting, and this itself can require risk-taking. Assessing new opportunities for play provision will entail risk-benefit assessment, consideration of standards and similar guidance, expert advice, experience from other locations and personal and collective experience. Even with all of this, decisions will still require judgement. For some schemes, the only way to test them will be to implement them and to monitor and evaluate their risks and benefits. But to achieve this, experts believe it is necessary for regulatory agencies, safety professionals, insurers, the courts and other interested parties to accept that duty holders are not necessarily blameworthy if these experiments have adverse outcomes.

A more forgiving society is required which admits that the health and welfare of children and young people is not synonymous with injury prevention, and that, while all reasonable safeguards should be put in place, what constitutes a reasonable balance is exceedingly difficult to forecast with any degree of certainty. As Rick Haythornthwaite of the Better Regulation Commission said in 2006: 'By allowing entrepreneurs and public servants to take risks, we must accept that they may make more mistakes' (Haythornthwaite, 2006).

There are benefits from this approach at all levels and for all those involved in play, but above all for the children, who will have happier and more satisfying experiences of childhood with richer opportunities for healthy growth and development into competent and confident adults.

References

Adams, J (1995) *Risk*. London: UCL Press.

Ball, D J (2000a) 'Ships in the night and the quest for safety'. *Injury Control and Safety Promotion* 7 (2), 83–96.

Ball, D J (2000b) Chapter 19 in McLatchie G, Harries M, Williams C and King J (2000) *ABC of Sports Medicine*. Oxford: BJM Books.

Ball, D J (2002) *Playgrounds – Risks, benefits and choices*, Sudbury: HSE Books.

Ball, D J (2004) 'Policy issues and risk-benefit trade-offs of "safer surfacing" for children's playgrounds', *Accident Analysis & Prevention* 35(4), 417–424.

Ball, D J (2007) 'Risk and the demise of children's play', Chapter 4 in *Growing Up with Risk*, Thom, B, Sales, R and Pearce J J (eds). Bristol: The Policy Press.

Better Regulation Commission (2006) *Risk, Responsibility and Regulation: Whose risk is it anyway?* London: Better Regulation Commission.

BSI (2006) *BS EN 14974: Facilities for users of roller sports equipment. Safety requirements and test methods.* British Standards Institution.

BSI (2007) *BS EN 15312: Free access multi-sports equipment. Requirements, including safety and test methods.* British Standards Institution.

BSI (2008a) *BS EN 1176-1: Playground equipment and surfacing – Part 1: General safety requirements and test methods.* British Standards Institution.

BSI (2008b) *BS EN 1177: Impact absorbing playground surfacing. Safety requirements and test methods.* British Standards Institution.

CEN (2006) *Guide 12: Child Safety: Guidance for its Inclusion in Standards.*

Children's Play Council (2006) *Planning for Play: Guidance on the development and implementation of a local play strategy.* London: National Children's Bureau and Big Lottery Fund [currently being revised by Play England].

DCSF (2007a) *The Children's Plan: Building Brighter Futures*. London: Department for Children, Schools and Families.

DCSF (2007b) *Staying Safe: A consultation document*. London: Department for Children, Schools and Families.

DCSF (2008a) *Staying Safe: Action Plan*. London: Department for Children, Schools and Families.

DCSF (2008b) *Fair Play: A consultation on the play strategy*. London: Department for Children, Schools and Families.

DfES (2006) *Learning Outside the Classroom Manifesto*. London: Department for Education and Skills.

DfT (2004) *Road Casualties Great Britain*. London: Department for Transport.

DTI (2005) *The General Product Safety Regulations* 2005: *Guidance for businesses, consumers and enforcement authorities*. London: DTI.

Eager, D, Nixon, J and Yearley, D (2008) 'Impact Attenuation: The case for natural materials', paper presented at International Play Association conference, Hong Kong.

Furze, A (2006) *In Praise of Playgrounds*, available online at the Association of Play Industries website: www.api-play.org/Archived-News-2006 (accessed 25 August 2008).

Gill, T (2006) *Growing Adventure: Final Report to the Forestry Commission*. Bristol: Forestry Commission.

Gill, T (2007) *No Fear: Growing up in a risk averse society*. London: Calouste Gulbenkian Foundation.

Graham, J D and Wiener, J B (1995) *Risk Versus Risk – Tradeoffs in protecting health and the environment*. Cambridge Mass: Harvard University Press.

GLA (2008) *Supplementary Planning Guidance: Providing for Children and Young People's Play and Informal Recreation*. London: Greater London Authority.

Goodridge, C edited by Douch, P (2008) *Inclusion by Design: A guide to creating accessible play and childcare environments*. London: KIDS.

Hackett, J, Chair of the Health and Safety Executive, speaking at an Institute of Occupational Safety and Health event, 8 May 2008; available online at:
www.hse.gov.uk/aboutus/speeches/transcripts/iosh080508.htm (accessed 2 September 2008).

Harrop, P (2006) *Rope swings, Dens, Tree houses and Fires: A risk based approach for managers facilitating self-built play structures and activities in woodland settings*. Bristol: Forestry Commission.

Haythornthwaite, R (2006) 'The regulation of risk – setting the boundaries' paper for University of Bath, Centre for Study of Regulated Industries, March 2006, 6.

HM Treasury (2003) *The Green Book: Appraisal and Evaluation in Central Government*. London: TSO.

HSE (2006) *Five Steps to Risk Assessment;* available online at the HSE website at
www.hse.gov.uk/risk/principlespoints.htm (accessed 25 August 2008).

HSE (2007) *Managing Health and Safety in Construction: Construction (Design and Management) Regulations 2007. (CDM) Approved Code of Practice.* Sudbury: HSE Books.

Hoffmann, Lord Leonard, H 'The Social Cost of Tort Liability', speech at National Constitution Centre, Philadelphia, USA, 27 June 2005; available online at: http://commongood.org/learn-reading-cgpubs-speeches.html (accessed 25 August 2008).

House of Lords judgment (2003) UKHL 47. Available online at: www.publications.parliament.uk/pa/ld200203/ldjudgmt/jd030731/tomlin-1.htm (accessed 25 August 2008).

Houston, L, Worthington, R and Harrop, P (2006) *Design Guidance for Play Spaces.* Available from the Forestry Commission website: www.forestry.gov.uk/england-play (accessed 25 August 2008).

Jarvis, S, Towner, E and Walsh, S (1995) Chapter 6 in *The Health of our Children – Decennial supplement*, Botting, B (ed). London: OPCS.

John, A and Wheway, R (2004) *Can Play, Will Play: Disabled children and access to outdoor playgrounds.* London: National Playing Fields Association.

Jones, M (2000) *A Textbook on Torts, 7th edition.* London: Blackstone Press.

Khambalia, A et al (2006) 'Risk factors for unintentional injuries due to falls in children aged 0–6 years: a systematic review', *Injury Prevention*, 12, 378–385.

Lester, S and Maudsley, M (2006) *Play Naturally: A review of children's natural play*, London: Play England/National Children's Bureau.

Manwaring, B and Taylor, C (2006) *The Benefits of Play and Playwork.* London: Skillsactive.

National Audit Office (2001) *Modern Policy-Making: Ensuring policies deliver value for money.* Report by the Comptroller and Auditor General, HC 289 Session 2001-2. London: Stationery Office.

NPFA, Children's Play Council and PLAYLINK (2000) *Best Play: What play provision should do for children.* London: National Playing Fields Association.

Norton C et al (2004) 'Playground injuries to children', *Archives of Disease in Childhood.* 89(2), 103-108

ODPM (2003) *Developing Accessible Play Space: A good practice guide.* West Yorkshire: Office of the Deputy Prime Minister.

PLAYLINK (1997) *Risk and Safety in Play: The law and practice for adventure playgrounds.* London: PLAYLINK.

PLAYLINK (2006) Negligence, play and risk – legal opinion, available online at: www.playlink.org.uk/articles/?p=8 (accessed 25 August 2008).

PLAYLINK (undated): Play policy development available online at: www.playlink.org/services/policy_and_strategy/play_policy_development.html (accessed 25 August 2008)

Play Safety Forum (2002) *Managing risk in play provision: A position statement.* London: National Children's Bureau (reprinted June 2008, available online at www.playengland.org.uk/resources).

PlayToday (2008) 'What are you playing at!', *PlayToday*, 62, May 2008.

Select Committee on Economic Affairs (2006) *Government Policy on the Management of Risk.* Downloadable as a pdf: www.publications.parliament.uk/pa/ld200506/ldselect/ldeconaf/183/183i.pdf (accessed 25 August 2008).

Shackell, A, Butler, N and Ball, D (2008) *Design for Play: A guide to creating successful play spaces.* London: Department for Children, Schools and Families, Department for Culture, Media and Sport and Play England.

Towner E et al (2001) *What works in preventing unintentional injuries in children and young adolescents? An updated systematic review.* London: Health Development Agency.

Welsh Assembly Government (2002) *Welsh Assembly Government Play Policy.* Available online at: www.wales.gov.uk (accessed October 2008).

Glossary

API	Association of Play Industries
BRC	Better Regulation Commission (reconstituted in 2008 as the RRAC)
BSI	British Standards Institution
CEN	European Committee for Standardisation (Comité Européen de Normalisation)
DCSF	Department for Children, Schools and Families
DDA	Disability Discrimination Act
HSC	Health and Safety Commission (merged with the HSE in 2008)
HSE	Health and Safety Executive
IAS	Impact attenuating surfacing
ISRM	Institute of Sport and Recreation Management
PSF	Play Safety Forum
RPII	Register of Play Inspectors International
RRAC	Risk and Regulation Advisory Council

Appendix 1:
Managing Risk in Play Provision:
A position statement

Summary statement

Children need and want to take risks when they play.
Play provision aims to respond to these needs and wishes
by offering children stimulating, challenging environments
for exploring and developing their abilities. In doing this,
play provision aims to manage the level or risk so that
children are not exposed to unacceptable risks of death
or serious injury.

This section contains the original text from the Play Safety Forum position statement *Managing Risk in Play Provision* published in 2002. This is not a summary of this implementation guide and is not a Government statement

play safety forum

'**We consider** *Managing risk in play provision* **to be an important document that will contribute to the debate on the provision of children's play.'** Health and Safety Executive

Introduction

The Play Safety Forum, a grouping of national agencies involved in play safety, has produced *Managing risk in play provision* to support the work of those involved in play provision of any kind – for example play areas, playgrounds, adventure playgrounds, play centres and holiday playschemes. These include local authorities, voluntary organisations, play equipment manufacturers and inspection agencies.

The statement has relevance to other settings and environments in which children play, such as childcare provision, schools, parks and public open spaces. It will also be of interest to those involved in insurance and litigation in relation to play provision. The statement has equal relevance to children and young people of all ages from birth to 18 years, and it uses the term 'children' to cover the whole age range. It focuses on physical injuries resulting from accidents. However, the overall approach, namely that a balance should be struck between risks and benefits, is also relevant to agencies concerned with other issues such as the personal safety of children.

The statement includes the summary (see page 114) and the following full statement. The summary aims to state the key points of the full statement in a more accessible form, for a non-technical audience.

Context

There is growing concern about how safety is being addressed in children's play provision. Fear of litigation is leading many play providers to focus on minimising the risk of injury at the expense of other more fundamental objectives. The effect is to stop children from enjoying a healthy range of play opportunities, limiting their enjoyment and causing potentially damaging consequences for their development.

This approach ignores clear evidence that playing in play provision is a comparatively low risk activity for children. Of the two million or so childhood accident cases treated by hospitals each year, less than two per cent involve playground equipment. Participation in sports like football, widely acknowledged as 'good' for a child's development, involves a greater risk of injury than visiting a playground. Fatalities on playgrounds are very rare – about one per three or four years on average. This compares with, for instance, over 100 child pedestrian fatalities a year and over 500 child fatalities from accidents overall. (Ball, 2002).

In response to this situation, and in order to ensure that children's needs and wishes are properly acknowledged, the Play Safety Forum has prepared this statement.

Managing risk in play provision Play Safety Forum statement

Acceptable and unacceptable risk

In any human activity, there is an element of risk. Three factors are central to determining whether or not the level of risk is acceptable or tolerable:

● the likelihood of coming to harm

● the severity of that harm

● the benefits, rewards or outcomes of the activity.

Judgements about the acceptability of risk are made on the basis of a risk assessment. Risk assessment and management are not mechanistic processes. They crucially involve making judgements about acceptability based on an understanding of the balance between risks and benefits. Even where there is a risk of fatal or permanent disabling injury, this risk may sometimes be tolerable. For instance, going paddling at the seaside involves an unavoidable risk of fatal injury, but this risk is tolerable for most people because in most circumstances the likelihood of coming to harm is very low and there are obvious benefits. Social and psychological factors are also important in risk assessment. Risks that are acceptable in one community may be unacceptable in another, and policies should take this into account.

Almost any environment contains hazards or sources of harm. In many cases the existence of hazards can be justified, perhaps because they are impossible to remove or perhaps because their removal would have undesirable consequences or be too costly. Where the existence of a hazard can be justified, measures should be in place to manage it. In a controlled environment such as a workplace or a playground, those responsible are required by law to identify, and make informed judgements about, the hazards to which people are exposed. They must take steps to ensure that the risks are managed and controlled so far as is reasonably practicable while allowing the potential benefits to be delivered.

Children and risk

All children both need and want to take risks in order to explore limits, venture into new experiences and develop their capacities, from a very young age and from their earliest play experiences. Children would never learn to walk, climb stairs or ride a bicycle unless they were strongly motivated to respond to challenges involving a risk of injury. Disabled children have an equal if not greater need for opportunities to take risks, since they may be denied the freedom of choice enjoyed by their non-disabled peers.

It is the job of all those responsible for children at play to assess and manage the level of risk, so that children are given the chance to stretch themselves, test and develop their abilities without exposing them to unacceptable risks. This is part of a wider adult social responsibility to children. If we do not provide controlled opportunities for children to encounter and manage risk then they may be denied the chance to learn these skills. They may also be more likely to choose to play in uncontrolled environments where the risks are greater.

Any injury is distressing for children and those who care for them, but exposure to the risk of injury, and experience of actual minor injuries, is a universal part of childhood. Such experiences also have a positive role in child development. When children sustain or witness injuries they gain direct experience of the consequences of their actions and choices, and through this an understanding of the extent of their abilities and competences. However, children deserve protection against fatal or permanently disabling injuries, to a greater degree than adults.

Children have a range of physical competences and abilities, including a growing ability to assess and manage risk, which adults arguably tend to underestimate. However, children typically have less experience than adults of assessing the broad range of risks and hazards that they may encounter. So it is important to give them appropriate controlled environments in which they can learn about risk.

Play provision and risk

Risk-taking is an essential feature of play provision, and of all environments in which children legitimately spend time at play. Play provision aims to offer children the chance to encounter acceptable risks as part of a stimulating, challenging and controlled learning environment. In the words of the play sector publication *Best Play*, play provision should aim to 'manage the balance between the need to offer risk and the need to keep children safe from harm'. While the same principles of safety management can be applied both to workplaces generally and play provision, the balance between safety and benefits is likely to be different in the two environments. In play provision, exposure to some risk is actually a benefit: it satisfies a basic human need and gives children the chance to learn about the real consequences of risk-taking.

Therefore it is acceptable that in play provision children may be exposed to the risk of minor and easily-healed injuries such as bruises, grazes or sprains. On the other hand, play provision should not expose children to significant likelihood of permanent disability or life-threatening injuries. However, it may on occasions be unavoidable that play provision exposes children to the risk – the very low risk – of serious injury or even death. But this would only be tolerable in the following conditions:

- the likelihood was extremely low
- the hazards were clear to users
- there were obvious benefits

● further reduction of the risk would remove the benefits

● there were no reasonably practicable ways to manage the risk.

For example a paddling pool, even if shallow, involves a very low but irremovable risk of drowning (even with parental supervision), but this is normally tolerable. The likelihood is typically extremely low; the hazard is readily apparent; children benefit through their enjoyment and through the learning experience of water play; and finally, further reduction or management of the risk is not practicable without taking away the benefits.

Providers should strike a balance between the risks and the benefits. This should be done on the basis of a risk assessment. Crucially, this risk assessment should involve a risk-benefit trade-off between safety and other goals, which should be spelt out in the provider's policy. Given children's appetite for risk-taking, one of the factors that should be considered is the likelihood that children will seek out risks elsewhere, in environments that are not controlled or designed for them, if play provision is not challenging enough. Another factor is the learning that can take place when children are exposed to, and have to learn to deal with, environmental hazards. Play provision is uniquely placed to offer children the chance to learn about risk in an environment designed for that purpose, and thus to help children equip themselves to deal with similar hazards in the wider world.

Good practice

Clear, well-understood policies, together with procedures that put these policies into practice, are the key to good practice in risk management in play provision. Policies should state clearly the overall objectives. Procedures, including risk assessment, should state how these policies are put into practice, giving guidance but also recognising the need for professional judgement in setting the balance between safety and other goals. Such judgements are clearly multidisciplinary in nature. For example, while they may contain an engineering dimension, a knowledge of child development and play itself is likely to be of equal or greater importance. The Children's Play Information Service has information on sources of authoritative, relevant guidance on good practice.

One valuable approach to risk management in play provision is to make the risks as apparent as possible to children. This means designing spaces where the risk of injury arises from hazards that children can readily appreciate (such as heights), and where hazards that children may not appreciate (such as equipment that can trap heads) are absent. This is particularly useful in unsupervised settings, where the design of the equipment and the overall space has to do most of the work in achieving a balanced approach to risk.

Ball, D (2002) *Playgrounds – risks, benfits and choices*, Contract Research Report No. 426/2002. Sudbury: HSE Books.

British Standards Institute (1998) BS EN 1176-1 Playground Equipment – Part 1. London: British Standards Institute.

Children's Play Council, National Playing Fields Association and PLAYLINK (2000) *Best Play: What play provision should do for children*. London: National Playing Fields Association

Conclusion

Safety in play provision is not absolute and cannot be addressed in isolation. Play provision is first and foremost for children, and if it is not exciting and attractive to them, then it will fail, no matter how 'safe' it is. Designers, managers and providers will need to reach compromises in meeting these sometimes conflicting goals. These compromises are a matter of judgement, not of mechanistic assessment. The judgements should be based on both social attitudes and on broadly-based expert opinion informed by current good practice. They should be firmly rooted in objectives concerned with children's enjoyment and benefit. And they should take into account the concerns of parents. Ultimately the basis of these judgements should be made clear in the policies of the play provider as written down in policy documents. These policies should in turn be understood and embodied in practice by all the key stakeholders.

'We consider *Managing risk in play provision* to be an important document that will contribute to the debate on the provision of children's play. It articulates the balance between the benefit and the need for children to play against the duty of play providers to provide safe play. It makes clear that the safety must be considered at all stages of play provision but that, inevitably, there will be risk of injury when children play, as there is risk of injury in life generally. We must not lose sight of the important developmental role of play for children in the pursuit of the unachievable goal of absolute safety. The important message, though, is that there must be freedom from unacceptable risk of life-threatening or permanently disabling injury in play.'

Health and Safety Executive

The Play Safety Forum

The Play Safety Forum brings together the main national organisations in England with an interest in safety and children's play. Members include representatives from providers, regulatory bodies and expert agencies. The aim of the Play Safety Forum is to build consensus on issues around risk and safety in relation to play provision. It is an independent body hosted by Play England.

Play Safety Forum members (February 2008)

Association of Play Industries
Child Accident Prevention Trust
Fields in Trust (formerly NPFA)
Institute of Sport and Recreation Management (ISRM)
KIDS (formerly KidsActive)
Play England (formerly Children's Play Council)
Play Scotland
Play Wales
Royal Society for the Prevention of Accidents (RoSPA)
SkillsActive
Local authority representatives

The Play Safely Forum is supported by:

Department for Culture, Media and Sport

In addition, the following were forum members when the position statement was first produced in 2002

Health and Safety Executive
Institute of Leisure and Amenity Management
Local Government Association
National Early Years Network
National Family and Parenting Institute
National Society for the Prevention of Cruelty to Children
PLAYLINK

Appendix 2: European playground equipment standards

BS EN 1176: 2008 Playground equipment and surfacing

Parts

This European Standard consists of a number of parts as follows:

EN 1176-1, *Playground equipment and surfacing — Part 1: General safety requirements and test methods.*

EN 1176-2, *Playground equipment and surfacing — Part 2: Additional specific safety requirements and test methods for swings.*

EN 1176-3, *Playground equipment and surfacing — Part 3: Additional specific safety requirements and test methods for slides.*

EN 1176-4, *Playground equipment and surfacing — Part 4: Additional specific safety requirements and test methods for cableways.*

EN 1176-5, *Playground equipment and surfacing — Part 5: Additional specific safety requirements and test methods for carousels.*

EN 1176-6, *Playground equipment and surfacing — Part 6 : Additional specific safety requirements and test methods for rocking equipment.*

EN 1176-7, *Playground equipment and surfacing — Part 7: Guidance on installation, inspection, maintenance and operation.*

EN 1176-10, *Playground equipment and surfacing — Part 10: Additional specific safety requirements and test methods for fully enclosed play equipment.*

EN 1176-11, *Playground equipment and surfacing — Part 11: Additional specific safety requirements and test methods for spatial network.*

EN 1176 should be read in conjunction with:

EN 1177: 2006, *Impact attenuating playground surfacing — Determination of critical fall height* (draft version of EN 1177: 2006 is currently in circulation, publication of final standard to be confirmed).

Introduction to EN 1176-1

It is not the purpose of the requirements of this standard to lessen the contribution that playground equipment makes to the child's development and/or play, which is meaningful from an educational point of view. This standard acknowledges the difficulties of addressing safety issues by age criteria alone because the ability to handle risk is based on the individual users' level of skills and not by age. Also users other than the intended age range will almost certainly make use of the playground equipment.

Risk-taking is an essential feature of play provision and of all environments in which children legitimately spend time playing. Play provision aims to offer children the chance to encounter acceptable risks as part of a stimulating, challenging and controlled learning environment. Play provision should aim at managing the balance between the need to offer risk and the need to keep children safe from serious harm.

The principles of safety management are applicable both to workplaces in general as well as to play provision. However, the balance between safety and benefits is likely to be different in the two environments. In play provision exposure to some degree of risk may be of benefit because it satisfies a basic human need and gives children the chance to learn about risk and consequences in a controlled environment.

Respecting the characteristics of children's play and the way children benefit from playing on the playground with regard to development, children need to learn to cope with risk and this may lead to bumps and bruises and even occasionally a broken limb. The aim of this standard is first and foremost to prevent accidents with a disabling or fatal consequence, and secondly to lessen serious consequences caused by the occasional mishap that inevitably will occur in children's pursuit of expanding their level of competence, be it socially, intellectually or physically.

Refusal of admittance and access as a safety precaution is problematic due to, for example, breach in supervision or help by peers. Requirements of significant importance, such as, for example, head and neck entrapment and protection against inadvertent falls, have been written with this in mind. It is also recognised that there is an increasing need for play provision to be accessible to users with disabilities. This of course requires play areas to provide a balance between safety and the offer of the required level of challenge and stimulation to all possible groups of users. However, for the purposes of protection against head and neck entrapment, this standard does not take into account children with an increased size of the head (e.g. hydrocephalus or Downs Syndrome) or wearing helmets.

Scope of EN 1176–1

This part of EN 1176 specifies general safety requirements for public playground equipment and surfacing. Additional safety requirements for specific pieces of playground equipment are specified in subsequent parts of this standard.

This part of EN 1176 covers playground equipment for all children. It has been prepared with full recognition of the need for supervision of young children and of less able or less competent children.

The purpose of this part of EN 1176 is to ensure a proper level of safety when playing in, on or around playground equipment, and at the same time to promote activities and features known to benefit children because they provide valuable experiences that will enable them to cope with situations outside the playground.

This part of EN 1176 is applicable to playground equipment intended for individual and collective use by children, but excluding adventure playgrounds. It is also applicable to equipment and units installed as children's playground equipment although they are not manufactured as such, but excludes those items defined as toys in EN 71 and the Toys Safety Directive.

NOTE Adventure playgrounds are fenced, secured playgrounds, run and staffed in accordance with the widely accepted principles that encourage children's development and often use self-built equipment.

This part of EN 1176 specifies the requirements that will protect the child from hazards that he or she may be unable to foresee when using the equipment as intended, or in a manner that can be reasonably anticipated.

Permission to reproduce extracts from BS EN 1176:2008 is granted by BSI. British Standards can be obtained in PDF or hard copy formats from the BSI online shop: www.bsigroup.com/Shop or by contacting BSI Customer Services for hardcopies only: Tel: +44 (0)20 8996 9001, Email: cservices@bsigroup.com.